ACCLAIM FOR THE "V

M000119524

"I love movies and ha~~ ~~~~~~~ ~~ ~ number of movie clubs, where the major conversation is about the story and how well everyone liked the movie. Bob Moss opened my eyes up to the complexity of film and what to look for while engrossed in a movie. The music, cinematography, lighting are a few of the areas that I now focus on when I am at the movies. I have also learned how to look for multiple themes. It has made my movie going a much richer experience."

- Debbra Lang

"I've 'watched' movies since I was 6 years old but have actually 'seen' films only since being made aware of what to look for in the frames. I've learned from Bob's provocative and challenging insights and examples of the elements essential to reaching the emotional and believable response the director strives for...from the actor and audience alike. His formula works for me!"

- Bobbi Meyers

"As I was reading *Vibes From The Screen*, I was upset at realizing all that I've been missing in films. Now I have a great guide to enrich my future film viewing. I will be approaching movies with a different mindset. I'm excited!"

- Shannon Lindsey

"Learning the elements of films has been enriching. At first, it might seem to some that it detracts from the viewing of the film as one consciously focuses on the music, cinematography, editing, etc. However, with practice, this becomes second nature and substantially increases one's appreciation of the film. As a couple, our post viewing discussions have become much more intense and interesting as we discover how the elements have clarified and magnified the character development and plot of the film. We are now more frequent movie-goers and can even appreciate movies that do not fit our previous criteria."

- Carol and John Rappel

"Bob Moss's popular 'Lunch Time at the Movies' has changed the way I approach movies—and for the better. Bob's way of coaching the group to inspect some key building blocks of each movie has helped me appreciate the importance and value of the various elements of a movie and also to seek out movies with potential strength in some of those areas. Before Bob's class, I thought of most movies in the dimension of how much I 'liked' them. Now, I try to see what parts of the movie I think are particularly well executed and how that affects me. Thanks, Bob!"

- Ted Davis

Vibes From The Screen

[signature]

August 2016

Vibes From The Screen

Getting Greater Enjoyment From Films

Bob Moss

MCP Books, Minneapolis, MN

MCP Books
322 First Avenue N, 5th Floor
Minneapolis, MN 55401
612.455.2293
www.mcpbooks.com

ISBN-13: 978-1-63505-065-3
LCCN: 2016908606

Distributed by Itasca Books

Cover Design by C. Tramell
Typeset by Robert Harmon

Printed in the United States of America

Dedication
To the memory of Roger Ebert

I did not know Roger Ebert. I had occasion to hear him speak about his art, but never had the honor of meeting him. That did not stop me from immediately feeling a terrible sense of loss upon hearing of his death; even three years later that feeling has not subsided. A Roger Ebert review provided not just his views on the quality and worth of the film in question, it was also a lesson on life. While Roger absolutely loved the art exhibited in a film, his reviews also related the emotions and reality found in the film. He frequently interjected his own life experiences when describing how the movie had affected him. He pointed out the lessons contained within the movie in plain, easily understandable language.

I learned how to appreciate the art found in film from Roger's writings. They taught me how to be more observant but, more importantly, how to let the film penetrate my outer barrier and reach my inner thoughts and feelings.

And so, on this the third anniversary of his death, it is with humble gratitude that I dedicate my effort to help others appreciate the art of film to the memory of the greatest film critic ever.

Bob Moss
April, 2016

Contents

Acknowledgments

I did not get this far on my own. Many, many people played a part in my developing this guide. Without their contributions and support the "vibes" may have stayed in the theaters. It started with my first film instructor at Northwestern University, R. Gabriel Dor, and was enhanced by the analytical challenges posed by Elliott Krick at The Graham School of the University of Chicago. Deepest thanks and kudos to my editor and guide Jill Welsh, who not only took my first drafts out of their morass but provided the strict guidance that I needed to focus my thoughts, and to publishing consultant Kim Bookless who was there through the course and quietly but directly enlightened me on the options so that I could make informed decisions. Without all of these people this book would never have gotten off the ground.

A special round of thanks must go the hundreds of members of my film study groups over the years at OLLI at Northwestern who not only showed me that the ideas worked but who constantly came up with new insights as we analyzed films together. *Vibes From The Screen* came about based upon our bi-weekly open discussions. A number of people provided feedback on various chapters along the way. Their comments honed my ideas. A particular acknowledgment, however, goes to OLLI member Joy Anderson who read each of the iterations of my manuscript, always providing cogent critique. I may not have always followed her advice but I at least had to think about why I was not doing so. Likewise OLLI members Carol and John Rappel were of great assistance in developing the film analyses contained in the book. I am truly thankful for the friendship and support of each and every member.

Several people have asked not to be identified for their contributions but I direct a big Thank You! to them.

Prologue

Art or Culture?

There was a time when films were not accepted as art. As the film industry grew it struggled to gain respect. Early movies were known as "photoplays" because people could only relate to them as an extension of the theater. The more these photoplays developed, however, the more it appeared their task was not simply to be an inexpensive imitation of the theater, but that they were an entirely new form of art. If they offer an art of their own, different from that of the theater, as the art of the painter is different from that of the sculptor, then it is clear one cannot be measured against the other. Who would say that a marble bust is a failure because it cannot show us the colors that give charm to the portrait painting?

Just as creating a paint color from a particular substance, or the different brush strokes artists use, or determining the substance upon which the paint is placed are each an art combined to provide the final piece of art, so too are the directing, acting, cinematography, editing, sound, etc., separate arts that combine to give us the glorious art of a film. A look at the credits rolling at the end of a movie gives us a slight idea of the hundreds of people and arts involved in the making of a movie. Acclaimed director Sidney Lumet's book *Making Movies* is, in my opinion, a must read for any true movie aficionado. It provides an introduction to both how movies are made and the intertwining of responsibilities of each department involved.

While some say theater is more true to life than film, I believe the opposite is true. In film we can see the entire picture straight through without having to wait for set changes. The camera glides through the entire scene and shows us the full spectrum. For example, it is not possible to get a close-up in the theater. Close-ups provide the audience with an intimacy with the characters. They also show the flaws in an actor's face or the sweat on their brows we would not see from most theater seats. For example, *The Nance* (2014), which is a filming of a live play, has a number of close-ups of Nathan Lane that, unfortunately, also show him sweating heavily from the extremely hot stage lighting. This resulting image distracts from Lane's moving performance.

The debate over whether or not film is "art" has raged for decades with the pendulum swinging freely. The early naysayers dismissed film as, at its best, a photographic record of an artistic performance, but not as an art form in its own right. This view conveniently ignores film techniques, such as the subtle lighting of actors' faces, the choice of colors in the frame, the angles of the shots, and the editing of the scenes for impact and transition—all of which assist in the communication of the message.

One of the problems was that there was no recognized definition of "art" as it related to film. What was necessary in the medium for it to be considered art? In his book, *It's Only a Movie*, Raymond Haberski provides an historical background. In the early 1900s the disagreement came down to cultural standards. At that time, art was owned by the rich and displayed by wealthy benefactors in museums located in the rich neighborhoods. Movies, on the other hand, were a popular culture, often shown together with vaudeville acts and ignored by the elitists. In a chapter entitled "Amusement or Art?" Haberski posits: "Most critics believed that motion pictures occupied the uncharted cultural space that lay between fine art and mindless entertainment. ...To the custodians of traditional culture, the popularity of motion pictures seemed particularly threatening to their authority to define what was good and what was vulgar."[1] Early movies, for the most part, were indeed vulgar by the day's standards, but could that alone prevent them from being art?

One of the arguments used against anything photographic being considered art was the claim that in order to be a representation of something, a piece must communicate thoughts about the subject depicted; it was not believed that photographs could be representational. These critics admitted that an artist can express thoughts by representing the subject in the painting in a particular way. The fallacy of their argument against including film as an art form is that films do the exactly same thing. The director presents the subject in a particular way, which may or may not be realistic, and guides the viewer to see the subject in the way he or she intends.

---

1 Raymond J. Haberski, Jr., *It's Only a Movie* (Lexington: The University Press of Kentucky, 2001), 10–11.

The following excerpt from an article by the distinguished director Ingmar Bergman provides a wonderful example of the communication of a picture:

"My grandmother had a very large old apartment in Uppsala. I used to sit under the dining-room table there, "listening" to the sunshine that came in the gigantic window. The bells of the cathedral went ding-dong, and the sunlight moved about and "sounded" in a special way. One day, when winter was giving way to spring and I was five years old, a piano was being played in the next apartment. It played waltzes, nothing but waltzes. On the wall hung a large picture of Venice. As the sunlight moved across the picture, the water in the canal began to flow, the pigeons flew up from the square, gesticulating people were engaged in inaudible conversation. Bells sounded, not from Uppsala Cathedral, but from the picture itself. And the piano music also came from that remarkable picture of Venice." [2]

In 1916, the German psychologist Hugo Münsterberg offered an alternative to both arguments, placing movies in the continuum of older art forms or those dismissing the photoplay as a tool of mass culture. To him it was "a unique inner experience that characterized the perception of the photoplays." Münsterberg marveled at the complex

---

2 Ingmar Bergman, "Why I Make Movies," September 1960 issue of *Horizon*.

environment created through a variety of techniques such as close-ups, flashbacks, dream sequences, multiple plots, and visual tricks. He thought photoplays illustrated how the mind created a narrative out of seemingly unrelated events and made associations out of a chaotic mass of images.[3] He saw movies as effecting culture, but not being the culture itself. If movies could require interpretation and evoke aesthetic reactions, then they had indeed become a distinct art form.

The addition of sound and color seemed to open the door for creative expression. *Don Juan* (1926) was the first major motion picture to employ a synchronized sound system throughout. Its soundtrack contained a musical score and sound effects, but no recorded dialogue, as it had been shot as a silent film. The first feature-length talkie was *The Jazz Singer* (1927). In the very early days, any color in film was hand painted onto the frames. *Cupid Angling* (1918) was the first color movie, meaning the colors were passed through the film and not painted onto it. Technicolor began to appear in the 1930s.

Many at the time believed that both sound and color slowed down the artistic progress of films. With sound present, actors did not have to convey as much through their acting, and many excellent actors were put out of work due to the sound of their voices. Likewise, color was initially seen as repressing the cinematographer's artistic skills. *The Artist* (2011), a black-and-white, silent film, was for

---

3 Hugo Münsterberg, *The Photoplay - A Psychological Study* (New York: D. Appleton and Company, 1916); Republished as *The Film-A Psychological Study* by Dover Publications Inc. in 1970.

a vast majority of the audiences their first exposure to that form of the art. The movie, its director, and the two leading actors won every major film award worldwide as the trade expressed its appreciation for the artistic expression.

The film-as-art movement took a big leap forward in 1933 when the director of the New York Museum of Modern Art (MoMA), Alfred Barr, hired a thirty-seven-year-old British film critic to be the museum's librarian. Iris Barry took on the challenge as submitted by Barr. Barr and Barry believed that those people with knowledge of great artists in painting and literature could learn to attain an equal knowledge of the comparable figures in film. They believed that MoMA could help cultured Americans respect filmmakers as they did other artists. By removing the elitist barrier and allowing for appropriate recognition, the way was paved for filmmakers to upgrade their craft and appeal to a broader range of the population.

In a 1938 article in *L'Écran francaise*, French critic and film director Alexandre Astuc propounded that: "The cinema is quite simply becoming a means of expression, just as all the other arts have been before it, and in particular painting and the novel. After having been successively a fairground attraction, an amusement analogous to boulevard theatre, or a means of preserving the images of an era, it is gradually becoming a language. By language, I mean a form in which and by which an artist can express his thoughts, however abstract they may be, or translate his obsessions exactly as he does in the contemporary essay or novel. That is why I would like to call this new age of cinema the age of camera-stylo (camera-pen)."

In the 1960s, as "art houses" began to take root in the United States, a distinction began to emerge in the minds of viewers and critics. "Movies" were disaster flicks, musicals, chick flicks, and the like, but "films" were art. This expression referred to French New Wave and other foreign films as well as some American films(such as *Easy Rider*, *Midnight Cowboy*, and others like them) that did not follow "the rules," but allowed the imaginations of the directors and the actors to flow freely on the screen.

> "We wanted messages and complexity and contradiction and most importantly, originality. We didn't care who the stars were. We learned through the jungle drums of the underground press what the heavy ones were, the must-sees whose power was not reflected in the *Variety* box office charts, but by the number of fellow hippies smoking dope in the theater."[4]
>
> —Michael Simmons, *Huffington Post*

French-Swiss director, screenwriter, and film critic Jean-Luc Godard once said, "The politics of a film is the budget of a film." Great artists take risks. But risk taking and experimentation are not always appreciated by the mass audiences. There is a certain level of intentional use of the viewers' brains that must occur, and the larger audiences just wanted to be entertained, be removed from life's reality

---

4 Michael Simmons, *HuffPost* "Entertainment," March 12, 2008 at http://www. huffingtonpost.com/michael-simmons/when-is-film-art_b_91225.html.

for an hour and a half with no effort required. The major studio bean counters only cared about the attendance; nothing else mattered.

In a 2013 speech on the "State of Cinema," director Steven Soderbergh stated: "Art is storytelling, and we need to tell stories to pass along ideas and information, and to try and make sense out of all this chaos. And sometimes when you get a really good artist and a compelling story, you can almost achieve that thing that's impossible which is entering the consciousness of another human being – literally seeing the world the way they see it. Then, if you have a really good piece of art and a really good artist, you are altered in some way, and so the experience is transformative and in the minute you're experiencing that piece of art, you're not alone. You're connected to the arts." [5]

A film's artistic value lies not in imitating other art forms, but in the uniqueness of film itself. Films can be aesthetically praised and also appreciated as independent art forms. Thus, the false distinction between movies and film falls when one recognizes that *all* motion pictures are art; some are good, some are bad, and a lot are in-between. But they are all art, nonetheless.

In 1997, Pulitzer Prize winning film critic Roger Ebert wrote a guest editorial for *The New York Times*, wherein he lobbied for the inclusion of film as an art worthy of receiving a Pulitzer Prize. To this day such has not occurred.

---

5 Steven Soderbergh, The State of Cinema, Delivered at the San Francisco International Film Festival on April 30, 2013. Video and transcript found at http://blog.sffs.org/home/2013/4/steven-soderbergh-the-state-of-cinema-video-tran-scripthtml.

Film, the Snubbed Art [1]
By Roger Ebert
CHICAGO

"The Pulitzer Prize is the most important award given to the arts in America. But movies, the most important art form in America, aren't eligible. It is time to change that. · · Pulitzer Prizes are awarded in two broad areas: for journalism, and for letters, drama and music. Movies encompass all three of the arts categories, and more.

Currently, nonjournalism prizes are given for fiction, drama, history, biography or autobiography, poetry, general nonfiction and music. But many Americans scarcely read a book a year, don't have the opportunity to see theater and do not often attend serious music. People do go to movies, and through television and home video, movies reach almost everywhere.

No other art form mobilizes a national discussion in such a big way. A "Pulp Fiction," "Hoop Dreams" or "Fargo" - even "The Full Monty" - can dominate conversations the way new plays or novels once did.

It is not hard to imagine why movies were excluded when the Pulitzer Prizes were first mapped out 80 years ago. At that time the founders would have remembered the earliest nickelodeon shows, when movies were hawked out of storefronts like sideshows. While movies

---

1 Guest Editorial - *New York Times*, October 22, 1997

had matured by 1917 - D.W. Griffith, Charlie Chaplin and Cecil B. De Mille were then in place - they were not completely respectable.

Perhaps they never will be. An art form will forever be in a separate category if you can attend it while eating Twizzlers. A Pulitzer student fellowship in film criticism is awarded every year, even though movies themselves aren't eligible for a prize.

Yes, we already have a lot of awards for movies. But a Pulitzer Prize would be valued because it would be awarded outside traditional industry-driven honors like the Oscars. Judges recommend winners, and the awards are evaluated by the Pulitzer board as a whole. This process can single out the kind of work that makes an impact without necessarily achieving great popularity.

A Pulitzer Prize, for example, might go to "Boogie Nights," which is likely to be passed over by the Academy Awards because of its disreputable subject matter, porn in the 1970s. Or it might go to a documentary like "Crumb," a portrait of how art barely saves a victim of a damaged family.

There is a renaissance now in American independent films. Theater chains are opening multiplexes to show them. Cable channels like Bravo, IFC and Sundance air them. But you won't find them "winning the weekend" at the box office. Winning a Pulitzer Prize, though, would generate bookings and audiences.

The Pulitzer board meets on Nov. 3 to discuss possible changes in its policies and additions to its categories: After a hundred years, movies deserve to be recognized."

Introduction

For as long as I can remember I have loved movies. Like most movie enthusiasts, I have my favorite genres and some that I truly dislike. The majority of films I see are somewhere in-between. As a college student I usually went to a movie theater at least every other week, and as my interest grew, it became every week. Now I try to see at least two to three new movies a week at theaters, in addition to those I watch at home.

At this point, I consider myself a movie aficionado and a student of film. Six years ago I decided to do something constructive with my love of films. So after forty years I went back to my university and took some basic film classes, where I learned more about how the various elements of film work to present the story. I followed up with study groups on interpretation, how to find the meanings contained within the movie. Then came the self-education process: reading, viewing, and attending lectures. I watched numerous interviews of directors, cinematographers, and actors, and I purchased educational DVDs produced by the Writers Guild, the Directors Guild, American Society of Cinematographers, and the American Film Institute.

Using Mark Cousins comprehensive exciting series *The Story of Film*, I began to learn the history of film. Through the video version, I also learned to recognize the "art" contained within each frame on the screen. I then progressed to teaching film to seniors (ages fifty to ninety+) at the Osher Lifelong Learning Institute (OLLI) at Northwestern University in Chicago and at private movie groups. My study groups have included classes on *The Art of Watching Films, Scene By Scene* (a BBC Series); *The Story of Film*; and a biweekly group called "*Let's Talk About the Movies,*" where we analyze new releases.

Today when watching films I realize how much more enjoyment I get from them. I enjoy being able to immediately identify why a particular piece of music was used or recognize a special technique I can feel affecting me. It is intellectually fulfilling for me to be able to discern deeper meanings from all of the techniques and clues contained within any film I watch. I wish to share some of this with you, the reader. This guide is just a beginning, and I hope it will encourage you to do some of your own self education.

During my film education I have read many books by and watched numerous interviews of screenwriters, directors, cinematographers and actors. I have also met some of these filmmakers while attending a number of film festivals. These experiences have always provided me with a better understanding and insight than purely academic, instructional material. Hence, you will find more than the usual number of quotes in this book. I see no reason to attempt to interpret or rephrase the wisdom and explanation provided by the filmmaking team members themselves. It is my belief that reading the filmmakers own words will assist you, the reader, to gain a better feel and understanding of how they think about their craft.

In order to analyze a film, it is important to understand the basic elements of film. It is not the intention of this book to be a training manual or film school text, but rather just to provide a sufficient explanation so that viewers can understand what is really happening on the screen as it was envisioned by the film's creators. For example, by understanding why the director used a particular camera angle, why certain music began at a specific point in a scene, or why the cinematographer chose a particular color or lighting effect in a scene, you will better be able to identify the messages conveyed. Always keep in mind that each element is an art unto itself.

> "One way of understanding better what a film is trying to say is to know how it is saying it."
> —Andre Bazin, French film critic

There are many other technical elements to filmmaking than those mentioned in this book, including, but not limited to, graphics, sound editing, costume, and set design. Each is an art unto itself and each, indeed, contributes to the viewer's perceptions and reactions. Not including them in this book's discussions does not diminish their important and vital role in a movie.

The discussions to follow address both feature and short films. Documentaries and most animated films are not addressed. There are many fine books about those types of films. Their examination requires a much different analysis.

As I stated above, this book is designed to be a basic guide, not a presentation of personal theory or a textbook. It is not intended for the casual film watcher nor is it for the film school student. It is for the cinephile and for the active film enthusiast. I believe that by understanding how filmmakers perceive and perform their jobs you will be aided in recognizing and appreciating the art they produce. That knowledge will enable you to view films with an understanding of what the filmmakers are trying to convey. I hope that by the end of reading this guide you will get up from viewing a film feeling the same type of excitement I do and the sense of having experienced something special.

PART ONE

Enjoying Films

CHAPTER ONE

Why People Watch Movies

Many people watch a movie purely for light entertainment. Others may hope to get something deeper out of the film, but lack the understanding and tools to see and absorb the art in front of them. Watching a film can be enhanced by viewing it with an informed awareness and some understanding of the elements of the craft of filmmaking. To gain the fullest appreciation, each film viewer should be receptive to the full experience mentally and emotionally. To view a film critically and elevate your viewing experience means to experience cinema with greater thought and awareness of your physical and emotional reactions.

I have discovered that the more one knows about filmmaking, the more one enjoys the art and begins to appreciate all of the effort put into the final cut. As you become more aware of the meaning(s) contained in a film, it will help you identify the common ground between you and the film.

People primarily watch movies for the experiences they provide:

1. They want a break from the daily grind and to be placed in a different situation. Some want the plain

escape to a mindless entertainment; others want emotional and mental stimulation.

2. A movie allows you to experience something that you cannot in your real life: for example, a way to fight back, a romance with a gorgeous partner, an adventure or trip, or being there in history.

3. For those two hours what is on screen seems real, and, as we absorb it, the art leads us to laugh, cry, learn, get scared, love, become aware, discover, be outraged, get confused, be disgusted, be touched, get sad, be distracted, be inspired, and many film viewers undergo what Samuel Taylor Coleridge called "the willing suspension of disbelief." They accept what is on the screen on its own terms, giving themselves over for a brief time to the face value of the director's depiction.

In describing how he approached thrillers, director Alfred Hitchcock believed that the less the hero of the play is emphasized, identified, and characterized, the more viewers will endow him/her with their own internal meaning and the more the viewer will identify with the character. In other words, by the filmmaker not placing an emphasis on any particular characteristic, the viewers are assured that *they* are like the hero.

We can all agree that movies allow us to escape, but it's often more than simple escapism. Movies can take us to places we've never been and inside the skins of people quite different from ourselves. They offer us a window into the wider world, broadening our perspectives and opening our eyes to new wonders. At the same time, a person can also choose not to watch some films for any number of reasons. It might be the genre, or a particular actor's presence, or a bias against the subject matter. Some people do not want to see particular movies because they can't or won't deal with the emotional reaction they fear may occur. Maybe the topic is too close to home, or they fear that the depicted events will happen to them. Many people over forty-five did not want to see *Still Alice* (2014) because it dealt with the early onset of Alzheimer's disease. The thought that they may possibly develop the disease was too much for those people to consider.

Movies help people fill some of their needs. The needs are individual in nature, and how the need is satisfied is individualistic. Some examples (all of which I have experienced):

- Movies are a way to acquire knowledge, information, and ideas.

- Movies feed into the moods of the viewers. Often they may provide a vehicle for release. Other times, they push an emotional button that has been suppressed. Have you ever watched a movie and then felt guilty because you had not done something in your life? Some films are feel-good movies, but others are sad, heavy movies.

- In a similar vein, sometimes we discover the capacity for pleasure from taboo activities in scenes we would never admit to in any other environment or time.

- People use media to reassure their status, gain credibility, and stabilize. "Compared to that family, I am really okay."

- Watching a movie with family or friends adds to your life enjoyment. If your friends are going to the movies you may also go to be part of the community discussion. Watching a movie on your own will probably let you pay more attention to the art of the film, but will leave you without the social venue necessary to think it all through afterward.

As British film professor Patrick Phillips has pointed out, we exit a movie wanting to talk and share impressions, sort out our reactions, and debate the film's issues and what it all meant. This is an integral part of our cinema visits.

C.S. Lewis, writing in *An Experiment in Criticism*, summarized our film-going purpose by stating that we "seek an enlargement of our being. We want to be more than ourselves. Each of us by nature sees the whole world from one point of view with a perspective and a selective-ness peculiar to himself... We want to see with other eyes, to imagine with other imaginations, to feel with other hearts, as well as with our own." [1]

Films use techniques, individually or combined, to convey both story and meaning. In their book *An Introduction to Film Analysis*, Michael Ryan and Melissa Lenos say that: "Whenever filmmakers lay out a set, direct actors to act in a certain way, place the camera in particular positions, and assemble the resulting mass of shots into a coherent narrative, they not only tell a story, they also make meaning." [2]

Even though the average moviegoer has viewed hundreds of films, the fundamental elements are not something they know much about. The goal of this book is to provide the reader with:

1.　an introductory understanding of basic film elements;

2.　a guide on how those elements are used within the film to convey a message to the viewer; and

3.　an understanding of how to discern any film's meaning.

It is my hope movie viewers will not only be more entertained, but by becoming more aware of the nuances and processes affecting their viewing pleasure, they will

---

1 C.S. Lewis, *An Experiment in Criticism* (New York: Cambridge University Press, 1961) 137-138.

2 Michael Ryan and Melissa Lenos, *An Introduction to Film Analysis* (New York: Continuum Int'l Publishing Group, Inc., 2012), 1.

be aesthetically stimulated and mentally challenged at the appropriate times. From those reactions will come an enhanced appreciation of the art.

Learning how to put this book's lessons to work will take time and effort on your part. My film-group members tell me that they initially became so involved in looking at the various elements of a film that they sometimes missed the overall experience. That is an unfortunate part of the learning curve that can be overcome. Many tell me they initially have to watch the movie at least twice to get both the entertainment value and enjoy the art. Unlike reading a book, where we can go back and reread a page or a chapter, a movie is running before your eyes at a certain number of frames per second. Unless you are watching a DVD that you can start and stop, movie viewing requires you to take it all in on the fly. This is why I urge people to give themselves time to fully process all that they have experienced at the viewing.

Slowly, my group participants become able to assimilate the two experiences into a single viewing. That being said, however, I always recommend watching a new movie at least twice. The second time may not be until it is released on DVD or TV but you will definitely find something new and gain even more understanding from the experience. There are some movies that I have enjoyed so much that I have watched them six or seven times over a number of years. Each viewing revealed something new and provided me a greater appreciation of the film and its art.

With the idea of keeping my study group members open to the full experience of a movie I have an important rule they must follow: NEVER read reviews before seeing a movie. Do not let yourself be influenced ahead of time either by the critics' various views of the storyline or their interpretations. To openly receive any movie, you must go in with no expectations. If you need something more than the description to decide whether or not to see a film, use the average ratings a film receives from a number of professional critics, which can be found on *Metacritic* or *Rotten Tomatoes* to guide you, but nothing else. Once you have seen the film then be sure to read some of the reviews and analyses to assist you in getting the fullest experience and understanding.

In order to appreciate the cinematic art of a film, it is necessary to open yourself up to receiving the physical and emotional vibes that emanate from the sounds, images, and action on the screen. This is something that can be cultivated, but it also requires frequent and varied film viewings and discussions. One frequent obstacle to becoming open is the viewer's past. Our personal experiences, education, and environments leave us all with an array of slanted opinions or biases. Learn to be flexible and how to judge the art objectively, which is not an easy task. One way to do this is to see as many different types and genres of film as possible.

It is important not to let your initial reaction control your ultimate understanding. Give yourself time to fully digest the combination of images and dialogue in any given movie before activating your own intellectualization, perceptions, and interpretations. This may take a few hours or a few days and, as said earlier, at least a second viewing.

Once you have read this book, there are some exercises you can do to help yourself become receptive to the fullest experience. They can be found in the Conclusion. In order to increase your appreciation of the art, you have to hone your attention, memory, and perception skills, which requires looking and listening closer than you may be used to doing.

"I took only one film course in my life... It was a course in film analysis, where [the teacher] would ask students to watch films and to concentrate on one specific element at a time: picture, sound, music, acting... Afterwards, everyone in the class would compare notes, and the things we discovered were pretty amazing. It was a fascinating course."
—David Lynch, director and screenwriter

CHAPTER TWO

How Films Influence the Viewers

What happens to us, the viewers, when we sit down to watch a film? How does a film influence the minds of different viewers? What are the mental processes that provide our experience of film? As early as 1916, Hugo Münsterberg laid out the basic processes at work: *perception*, *attention*, *memory*, *imagination*, *suggestion*, and *emotion*.[1] Today, all directors are cognizant of the fact that every film requires the viewer to use many senses, such as visual, auditory, spacial, temporal, and even sensory, and assimilate them into a unique experience. From this multiple stimulation comes enjoyment or dissatisfaction with the finished product.

Detailing how a movie must accomplish each of the processes he believed were required, Münsterberg stated:

"The mere perception of the men and women and of the background, with all their depth and their motion, furnishes only the material. The scene which keeps our interest alive certainly involves much more than the simple impression of moving and distant objects. We must accompany those sights with a wealth of ideas. They must have a meaning for us, they must be enriched by our own

---

1 Münsterberg, *The Photoplay - A Psychological Study.*

imagination, they must awaken the remnants of earlier experiences, they must stir up our feelings and emotions, they must play on our suggestibility, they must start ideas and thoughts, they must be linked in our mind with the continuous chain of the play, and they must draw our attention constantly to the important and essential element of the action."[2]

Many years later, Münsterberg's notion was supported by director George Stevens, who believed everything that went into a picture affected the viewers, although viewers don't realize the impact of tiny, minor things as they are revealed. They, nevertheless, have a great effect by working upon the subconscious.

Director Rob Reiner has stated that his goal is for the viewers of his movies to be unaware of any of the elements at work. Rather he wants the viewers to assimilate them all and let themselves be transported into the world of the film. Reiner goes on to say that he attempts to put the camera where the audience is so the audience is in the best position to get the information he wants them to receive.[3]

But does the director's perception matter? And whose perception ultimately counts? As will be seen in a later section, actors often have a different perception of their characters than the director, and it is usually their portrayals that win out. Likewise, in the end, the audience's perception may not match that of the director due to their

2 Ibid., 31.

3 Turner Movie Classics, "AFI Master Class: The Art of Collaboration – Rob Reiner and Robert Leighton," 2014.

own life experiences. If such an audience member still takes something significant from the film, has the director done his/her job? I believe so.

The meaning we take from a film is influenced in part by where our attention is drawn: voluntarily or involuntarily, both on the screen and coming from the speakers on the wall. These are the ways filmmakers can influence us. They hopefully provide a visceral, emotional, or mental reaction. To fill in the rest, the filmmaker must rely upon the viewer's imagination, perception, personal interests, and life experiences. It is this interaction with contributions by both the filmmaker and the viewer that leads to finding meaning in a film. To put it another way, a director can attempt to convey a certain message and meaning by controlling the film's elements, however the meaning a viewer takes away also depends upon the viewer's personal experiences and beliefs.

At a stage performance, the audience's perception is affected, to some extent, by where the person is sitting in the auditorium. At the movies, however, the picture on the screen is the same regardless of where the viewer is seated. A noted film critic was rumored to say that he liked to sit in the back on the left side of the auditorium, because it gave him the fullest view of the screen, and the director usually sat next to the left of the camera in the old days. But then along came computers and monitors, and today the director of a film shooting in digital sits at a table watching the action on the monitor and sees exactly what the audience will see on the movie theater screen. It is the

angle of the camera that matters, not the viewing angle of
the moviegoer.

Prior to the digital age, a film was composed of
hundreds of still frames that were passed in front of a light
on a projector at a fast speed. This created the illusion of
motion. To the viewer this sense of motion was real, yet
it was only created by the viewer's perception. Film, even
today, is a flat image, yet the viewer perceives depth. Such
impressions of depth are created by the manipulation of
the camera and our mental processes. Contrast these with
an audience member's view of a play in the theater, where
the movement and depth are real and do not require
additional enhancement by our minds.

In order to begin analyzing the art of a film, the viewers
should be aware at some point—even if it is after the movie
is over—that they were indeed influenced by the angle of
the shot, the depth, the lines of the photo, the shading of
the light, the shadows, the softness of part of the screen and
the sharpness of other parts, the music, the dialogue and
the editing. Each of these is an artistic element produced
by a specialist that attempts to influence one or more of the
interrelated, coordinated actions providing the physical,
mental, and visceral experiences encountered when
watching a movie:

1.   Whatever is attracting our attention enters into
     part of our consciousness and becomes clear.

2.   We experience a lack of attention to everything
     else.

3. We adjust our eyes, our ears, our body, our emotional level in order to let ourselves receive the fullest impression.

4. Our ideas, feelings, and impulses become focused around whatever our attention is being drawn.[4]

If we begin viewing the movie when we are upset, angry, or in any other type of highly emotional state, one of two things can happen: either we let the four actions begin to work and the experience is enjoyable, or we permit an emotional state to dominate and block the processes from occurring.

None of these processes can help us without memory. For each successive shot and scene to have meaning, the viewer must remember the previous shots and the prior scenes. Through the images, dialogue, music, and other sounds, the movie can suggest to our memory what it needs to recall. But a movie director has one tool a theater stage does not. The director can insert a quick flashback of a past scene at any time. Regardless of how quickly it happens, it is still effective. Whereas the close-up helps direct our attention, the flashback helps direct our memory. These are the marvels of the union of film technique and viewers' mental functions.

In *Short Term 12* (2013) the process occurs somewhat in reverse. At one point in the movie one of the patients, Jayden, is sitting in the community room waiting for her

---

4 Münsterberg, *The Photoplay - A Psychological Study*, 36–37.

father to pick her up. The TV is playing, and Jayden is casually watching. Suddenly, she jumps up and runs to her room. We are not sure what set her off. The TV was showing a cartoon about sharks. Later in the movie, Jayden is talking with the counselor and tells her a story about a shark eating an octopus bit by bit. The counselor and audience immediately realize that, through her story, Jayden is trying to tell the counselor that she has been sexually abused. Instantly, our memory lets us understand the earlier scene and why the young girl became so upset.

Sometimes the filmmaker leaves it to the viewers' imagination to fill in part of the story. Perhaps we must imagine what happened prior to what we are now viewing. This creates a level of suspense and desire to learn the facts—a tension that carries us through until the filmmaker is ready to pull back the curtain. Other times we are given the opportunity to imagine what might occur next or into the future. The way a film leads us to these imaginative moments can greatly affect not only our perception but, more importantly, our enjoyment and understanding of the film.

One of the questions often asked is why the viewer should care what happens to a character. If it is a nonfiction movie based on actual events, we already know the result. The movie is telling the tale about how the character(s) reached the ending. If it is a fictional story, the characters are not real, so why should their fate matter? What makes these fictional characters mean something to us?

We care about what happens because we identify with one or more of the characters. It doesn't seem to matter how the actor portrays the character. Once we identify with them, once we decide they are like us, we can let ourselves be carried by the film right into the middle of the scene. We are no longer objective observers.

In learning to **Appreciate the Art**, the viewer should inquire as to what it is in the movie that:

Grabbed their attention,

Stimulated their memory, and

Put their imagination to work.

The second part of that inquiry is determining which elements the filmmaker used to bring each of these about.

CHAPTER THREE

Film Genres

The movie a viewer chooses to watch often depends on its genre. Elements of some genres appeal to us, while others repel us. A genre is a recognized, defined group of films in which the stories are told in accordance with certain characteristics or conventions, as well as presentation modes—all of which are accepted by both filmmakers and audiences. When broken down to its roots, a genre provides a predictable structure in which to tell a particular type of story.

There are many genres coming out of Hollywood, including westerns, film noir, science fiction/fantasy, war stories, horror flicks, comedies, musicals, romances, and mysteries. The audience enters a movie in any genre with a preconceived notion of what is coming: the general storyline, the types of characters, the time period, and the settings, for example.

Most films in a particular genre have similar themes and character types. There is a basic pattern and the same general ingredients. Screenwriters today, though, do try to create some uniqueness within the constraints of the convention. One film theorist suggested that the popularity of genre films was, in part, due to the fact they hold out basic American beliefs and values. Because the conventions are already established, the director has a simplified task in the storytelling. The more notable directors tend to find creative variations and go outside of the box to give their films a unique, fuller, and identifiable style.

"**Action** films usually include high energy, big-budget physical stunts and chases, possibly with rescues, battles, fights, escapes, destructive crises (floods, explosions, natural disasters, fires, etc.), non-stop motion, spectacular rhythm and pacing, and adventurous, often two-dimensional 'good-guy' heroes (or recently, heroines) battling 'bad guys' - all designed for pure audience escapism. A major sub-genre is the disaster film.

Adventure films revolve around the conquests and explorations of a protagonist. The purpose of the conquest can be to retrieve a person or treasure, but often the main focus is simply the pursuit of the unknown. These films generally take place in exotic locations and play on historical myths. Adventure films incorporate suspenseful puzzles and intricate obstacles that the protagonist must overcome in order to achieve the end goal.

Comedies are light-hearted plots consistently and deliberately designed to amuse and induce laughter through exaggeration of the situation, the language, action, relationships and characters.

Crime (gangster) films are developed around the sinister actions of criminals or mobsters, usually underworld figures, or ruthless hoodlums who operate outside the law,

Dramas are serious, plot-driven presentations, portraying realistic characters, settings, life situations, and stories involving intense character development and interaction. Dramatic biographical films (or "biopics") are a major sub-genre, as are 'adult' films (with mature subject content).

Epics take historical events and people and interprets them in a larger scale. Historical accuracy is not the main focus in Epics, but rather the telling of a grandiose story. The drama of an Epic film is often accentuated by a sweeping musical score, lavish costumes, and high production value.

Horror films are designed to frighten and to invoke our hidden worst fears, often in a terrifying, shocking finale, while captivating and entertaining us at the same time in a cathartic experience. Horror films feature a wide range of styles, from the earliest silent Nosferatu classic, to today's CGI monsters and deranged humans. They are often combined with science fiction when the menace or monster is related to a corruption of technology, or when Earth is threatened by aliens. The fantasy and supernatural film genres are not usually synonymous with the horror genre. There are many sub-genres of horror: slasher, teen terror, serial killers, zombies, Satanic, Dracula, Frankenstein, etc. See Filmsite's Scariest Film Moments and Scenes collection - illustrated.

Musical/dance films are cinematic forms that emphasize full-scale scores or song and dance routines in a significant way. Major subgenres include the musical comedy or the concert film.

Sci-fi films are often quasi-scientific, visionary and imaginative - complete with heroes, aliens, distant planets, impossible quests, improbable settings, fantastic places, great dark and shadowy villains, futuristic technology, unknown and unknowable forces, and extraordinary monsters ('things or creatures from space'), either created by mad scientists or by nuclear havoc.

War (and anti-war) is a genre concerned with warfare, typically about naval, air, or land battles in the twentieth century, with combat scenes central to the drama. The fateful nature of battle scenes means that war films often end with them. Themes explored include combat, survival and escape, sacrifice, the futility and inhumanity of battle, the effects of war on society, and the moral and human issues raised by war. The stories told may be fiction, historical drama, or biographical.

Westerns are the major defining genre of the American film industry - a eulogy to the early days of the expansive American frontier. They are one of the oldest, most enduring genres with very recognizable plots, elements, and characters (six-guns, horses, dusty towns and trails, cowboys, Indians, etc.). Over time, westerns have been redefined, re-invented and expanded, dismissed, re-discovered, and spoofed."[1]

Some film genres are similar in nature with the major distinction being the setting. Compare the following:

A western's theme, which is the struggle of civilization and community versus the wilderness and lawlessness, with gangster movies that move the crime to an urban setting. Films in the gangster genre usually focus on a career criminal who rose from humble, meager surroundings to become the feared leader of a special community. The story proceeds, along with a lot of violence, in the struggle for power until the loss of power and violent death of the subject gangster. More recent gangster movies added ethnicity to the gangs.

Although not included in the list, film noir is considered a genre by some. It is a film movement that grew out of the gangster movies, and many scenes either have dark,

1 Source- Tim Dirks, *Main Film Genres*, www.filmsite.org

shadowy lighting or take place night, which accounts for its name. The characters are motivated by selfishness or greed and are willing to do almost anything to get whatever it is they want. Early film noir usually had a weak male led by a scheming female to break his sense of morality. The "femme fatale" was sexy, manipulative, and smooth talking; she used the weaker men to get what she wanted and then lured the man to his death.

When the Movie Picture Production Code was in effect (1930–1968), the villains were not allowed to "get away with it." They had to be killed or captured. The message that "crime does not pay" was a requisite for movies in western, gangster, and film noir genres.

With the technological advancements in the graphic and special-effects areas, science fiction and fantasy films have encountered a rebirth, and their popularity has grown immensely. These films offer the excuse to dream. The audience knows from the start that what they are about to see is not real. Audience members are emboldened by the thought that someday it might be possible to have the super powers that the movie's characters possess.

Although a rarity today, musicals were Hollywood extravaganzas at their best. Historian Rick Altman has written extensively on film musicals and has concluded that they come in three categories: the "show" *(Gypsy)*, the "fairytale" *(Shrek)*, and the "folk" *(Inside Llewyn Davis)*. Whatever the category, most musicals were feel-good movies; as the song goes, they accentuated the positive. The combination of drama and music goes back to Aristotle and ancient Greece. Today, in most musicals, the narrative is just a pretext—a bridge between musical numbers.

Genre classification provides a starting point in developing your film analysis. The same event depicted as a comedy will have a much different meaning than if that event is found in an drama or action film.

CHAPTER FOUR

Significant Differences Between European and American Films

Music Box Theatre, Chicago: © Robert Moss 2012

In one sense, the way to watch foreign-language films is no different than how you watch American movies. Look for how the director uses the key elements to convey a message. The filmmakers are still trying to manipulate you and direct your attention by using the same elements. It is the manner in which they use them and the storytelling that is significantly different. For some people, having to read the subtitles becomes a distraction, but one that can be overcome. The trick is to let the sound provide the pace and intonation as you read. Sit further back from the screen so that your head is not going from side to side while you read. Eventually, you will not notice you are reading subtitles. In your head, you will hear the words being said in the actors' tones, and they will meld with the images.

The key differences between European and American films are:

1. plot development and the timing of the story and

2. the purpose of the film.

Some would say that a major difference between European and American cinema is that European films have almost no plot and become cinematic essays, whereas American scriptwriters are taught that their films must have carefully prepared plots that the studio bosses can understand. Noted American critic Andrew Sarris once said that the difference between American movies and European films is that American movies tend to correspond to reality, while European films tend to comment on reality.

A serious distinction that affects the types of movies made is the fact that American films are producer controlled, while European films are director controlled. In the majority of the European films, the directors try to create something new and more artistic, and they take risks and expose themselves. That is rare in the United States. In what film theorist David Bordwell has called the "classical Hollywood style", the rules:

1. set stringent limits on individual innovation;

2. call for the production of a realistic, comprehensible, and unambiguous story; and

3. use artifice through techniques of continuity and invisible storytelling, which is the opposite of European filmmaking.

Award-winning European films, such as *The Artist*, *Amour*, and *Ida*, would never have been made in the U.S., let alone distributed. Getting them distributed in the U.S. was an exceptional feat for the filmmakers. The distributors that did gamble on these films reaped huge dividends.

Studio head Samuel Goldwyn once said, "Pictures are for entertainment, messages should be delivered by Western Union." As discussed earlier, Americans go to the movies to be entertained. They do not like having to think a lot as they watch the film and rarely think about its messages or meaning after leaving the theater. European films, however, require constant attention and a good memory. Their goal is to make you think. Generally speaking, American films rely on the foundation of a strong story and the ongoing plot development. American viewers expect fluid dialogue from characters with whom they can identify and adherence to genre standards. With European films, the necessity to be open to the film and let yourself feel it with no expectations, as I explained in the introduction, becomes even more important.

When viewing a European film, the viewer should pay attention to body language and facial expressions. Silence is seen as a virtue. American films, on the other hand, talk and keep talking. Characters are more prone to explain their feelings through the dialogue. In the 2001 French film *Intimacy*, a man and woman meet once a week for anonymous sex. No names, no small talk. They meet, have passionate sex on the floor and then they part. Director Patrice Cherau says, "But they are talking. It's the language of their bodies, and it's beautiful to watch." In the Polish film *Ida* (2014), the lead character, Anna (Ida), never says what she is thinking. Her face, eyes, and body tell it all, and, again, it is accomplished beautifully. There is no "spell-it-out" dialogue to tell Ida's story. The viewer must watch closely, interact with the film, and learn.

Comedies don't play well overseas in either direction because cultural sensibilities are much different. Humor tends to be more verbal, and the nuances that really make the comedy get lost in the translations. The theme for a comedy is usually obvious to the culture in which it was made with few, if any, subthemes. The pace is quick with a lot of close-up shots.

In telling of the impact Polish cinema has had upon him, Martin Scorsese recently stated, "With Polish cinema, what I especially respond to is the mixture of passion, meticulous craftsmanship, dynamic deep focal-length compositions, moral dilemmas and religious conflicts, often done with a very sharp sense of humor. Humor and tragedy are very close in Polish cinema.

"Plus, the struggle against official censorship and government clampdowns gives Polish cinema that was made during the communist era a heightened urgency. You can feel it in the rhythm, the intensity, even in pictures that have no obvious political subject matter."[1]

Famous British actor Jeremy Irons is less kind about Scorsese or American film. In answer to questions put to him during an interview by Gitte Nielsen, Irons explained his feeling about American films thusly:

"[I had just seen] *Goodfellas*, Scorsese's movie. I thought: Well that's great. He's a great movie-maker, knows how to use light, how to use the camera, how to tell a great story. And yet I don't feel anything. I don't feel anything. And I thought: some American movies – I know, it's a generalization – are like really good hookers. You know, they're expensive, they look great, they'll do anything you ask them to do, they'll give you a great time. And at the end of it

1 Martin Scorsese, "My passion for the humour and panic of Polish cinema," *The Guardian*, April 16, 2015.

you walk away and you think, [he makes a belittling gesture]. The other sorts of women are real women who maybe don't look as good as a hooker, who have their own ideas, who won't do everything you ask, who maybe don't cost you so much. But who you spend time with. And when you leave them, you can't get them out of your head." [2]

Danish director Jon Bang Carlsen points out that the "New Wave" directors[3] such as Resnais, Truffaut, and Godard, would never have a chance in the United States because they portray our existence as something that is sometimes inexplicable. Joining Irons in his assessment, Carlsen says:

"In the States they try to make more of an adrenaline injection of drama to get you hooked for an hour and a half; but right after that, you are supposed to be ready for the next film, so they want you to digest what you just saw rapidly to be ready to buy tickets for a new movie. That is my big problem with American films. They easily make me cry, but once I leave the cinema it never really touches me or connects with my life. It doesn't teach me anything. It never broadens me as a person."[4]

---

2 *p.o.v.* Danish Journal of Film Studies, no. 12, December, 2001, 5.

3 The French New Wave was a group of trailblazing French directors who exploded onto the film in the late 1950s and revolutionized cinematic conventions.

4 *p.o.v.* a Danish Journal of Film Studies, no. 12, December, 2001, 8.

Recently in articles in *The Independent*, a British newspaper, two American actor/directors have been critical of cinema in the United States. Michael Douglas spoke out against American actors' obsession with social media. Douglas believes that talent will suffer as a consequence.

"There's something going on with young American actors – both men and women-because Brits and Australians are taking many of the best American roles from them. Clearly it breaks down on two fronts. In Britain they take their training seriously while in the States we're going through a sort of social media conscious thing rather than formal training. Many actors are getting caught up in this image thing which is going on to affect their range."[5]

A few days earlier, Hollywood great Dustin Hoffman discussing the state of cinema lamented that "...I think that it is the worst that film has ever been – in the 50 years that I've been doing it, it's the worst."[6] Hoffman places part of the blame on directors being pressured to finish movies in very short time periods. Because of budget restraints and the greater use of technology many films are being shot in less than a month, compared to months or more in the past.

I make it a point to keep my film watching diverse, seeing not only European and American movies but also those from the Middle East and Far East. I lean toward European films because a) they are more likely to openly show and talk about controversial or taboo subjects; b)

---

5 "Michael Douglas: Social media obsession is to blame for crisis in young American actors," *The Independent*, July 8, 2012.

6 "Dustin Hoffman interview: The Graduate talks decline of cinema, difficulties finding work and wanting to be a jazz pianist. *The Independent*, July 3, 2015"

they provide deeper and more complex stories; and c) the usually understated acting seems more realistic and leaves room for more interpretation. I watch many French and Italian films, which tend to focus more on questions about existence or life in general while providing more intimate looks. The character's personas are not necessarily revealed by their actions in the early stages of the film. Most American films often do not allow the viewer the opportunity to experience the intricate weaving of the story, preferring to lay it out directly.

So, when viewing a European film, sit back and let the film carry you through the twists and turns and roundabouts the story takes. Do not try to guess what will happen or expect it to follow American norms. See if you are able to identify the difference in the filmmaking style from the American films you view. Which style do you appreciate more?   Which style leaves you feeling as if you have experienced or accomplished something really different?

Savor the art!

PART TWO

Film Elements

CHAPTER FIVE

The Story

For many people the first thing they consider when discussing a film and its art is the story. The film's concept may come from a producer, an independent screenwriter, a director, or an actor, but the actual story will be either an adaptation of another work or an original screenplay written by one or more screenwriters. Often the director is one of the screenwriters.

An original script is generally approximately 120 pages, which runs approximately two hours. During the filmmaking process, the script will get cut or expanded to fit the budget or the director's view. American screenwriters will tell you that the first ten pages are the foundation of the movie. During this time both the theme and tone of the movie is set, and the audience becomes comfortable with what is about to come.

The *theme* is the central focus of a film. It is the means by which the director communicates all that he/she offers the viewers. The theme may be found through a plot or series of subplots, characters and their traits, ideas espoused directly or implicitly, and perhaps even through the emotions expressed.

Although there is no set definition for *tone* within the industry, it is generally thought to be the story's relationship to reality. Another definition by Laura Schellhardt is: "A certain quality, mood or atmosphere that the writer establishes through the careful manipulation of the pace, texture and selected images....Tone can be understood as the way a movie makes you feel as you watch it."[1] Some writers set the tone as they begin writing. Others report that the tone comes about due to circumstances, either narrative or technological, that arise as they develop their characters.

The theme will have an effect on the tone of a film. Different movie themes and genres play at different speeds. For example, the slower a theme progresses, the more time is allowed for the emotional response to take effect and be noticed. In many foreign films the theme is not obvious until much later in the film. Foreign films do not reveal where they are going in that first ten-minute segment like most American films do. The viewer must pay close attention all the way through. Even foreign comedies have a level of suspense.

The *plot* is a series of events deliberately arranged to reveal their dramatic, thematic, and emotional significance. It is the specific actions and events selected by the filmmakers and arranged in a specific order so those events and actions will effectively convey the movie's narrative to a viewer. The movie's *narrative* is the story as a series of events recorded in chronological order. A good plot is necessary to tell a good story; however, the reverse is not true. A good story will not necessarily lead to a good plot.

---

1 *Notes on Craft: Mood, Tone and Voice*, *Writers Guild of America* (2009 DVD) quoting *Screenwriting for Dummies* by Laura Schellhardt (2008).

Film *auteur*[2] Jean-Luc Godard has said, "All movies have a beginning, a middle and an ending but not necessarily in that order." In essence, movies do have three acts, even if there is no curtain or discernible fade between them. Some movies start at the end and then go back to the beginning. Some start in the middle and eventually tell you what happened earlier.

Some screenwriters talk about getting into trouble somewhere in the middle of the script. They immediately go back to the first ten pages and either refresh their mindset or rewrite the beginning to fit where the story has gone during the writing process.[3] The next time you feel a movie dragging and start to look at your watch, pay attention to where the movie is in terms of time. It will probably be somewhere between half and two-thirds over, which means it is in the second act. Screenwriters say that one of three things occurred:

a)   The screenwriters started to get lost and didn't go back to their outline and rebuild.

b)   The director insisted on adding something in because he/she didn't feel the script conveyed the desired message.

---

2 According to François Truffaut, one of the leaders of the French New Wave, what made a director an "autuer" was that they were true creators with their passion and personality clearly seen throughout their movies. Because of this one could identify the director by what was on screen.

3 *Notes on Craft: Mood, Tone and Voice*, Writers Guild of America DVD, 2009.

   c)   The story became convoluted during the editing
       process.

Regardless of the reason, it is ultimately the director's fault for letting the situation remain in the final cut. Oscar-winning director John Schlesinger (*Darling*, *Midnight Cowboy*, *Sunday Bloody Sunday*) once said during an interview: "One sets out to make a film because one likes the subject matter. I believe the script is never finished. I constantly work on the script, either with the writer, or, if the writer is not there, with another writer, or with the people that are working with me. I think the script is the blueprint and then it has to have a life of its own."[4]

In the fourth century B.C., Aristotle in his Poetics laid out six required elements of drama: *plot*, *character*, *theme*, *dialogue*, *rhythm (music)*, and *spectacle*. Screenwriters still believe that each of those elements is necessary for successful films today. Hence, the starting point of a film is a script containing all of them. However, regardless of how the story comes across to you, what your feelings are toward a character, which of your emotions is triggered, what message you take away at any point in the film, and what you remember as you go about your life—are all dependent on many factors. It is not only how the story is written, but also

   •   how a character is portrayed by the actor;

4 Quoted at *The Film Director* on filmmakers.com. http://www.filmmakers.com/features/film/director2.htm.

- the lighting used;

- the camera angle and focus length;

- which music is used and when; and

- the other sounds present in the film.

Each of the artists responsible for these film elements can only go so far on their own. It is the director, with the assistance of the film editor, who must mix them in the proper proportion to create the sounds and images the viewer receives and takes into their experience. But, as the viewer, it is possible to walk away with greater appreciation and enjoyment from any one of these elements even when you may not like the whole. That is the essence of appreciating the art of film.

The Story: Appreciating the Art
Ask yourself the following questions after viewing a film:

- Can I identify the manner in which the theme is expressed? Is it via a plot, a character, a nonhuman object?

- Is there a strong structure? Does the story fit together and does it hold throughout?

- Does the texture of the story aid the viewer in understanding the story?

- Do both story and plot exist?

- Is there a definitive point of view, or does it change as the movie progresses?

- Was the apparent goal of the writer accomplished?

- Did the mood and tone have an effect upon me?

- Did I identify and relate with any character?

CHAPTER SIX

Visual Effects

Special effects is a term generally used to describe all simulated illusions in the film, television, and entertainment industries. Special effects, as we know them today, are traditionally divided into the categories of scenery effects, mechanical effects, and visual effects. Visual effects (FX) is the term generally associated with the integration of live-action footage with computer-generated imagery (CGI), such as animation and compositing.

Visual or special effects have been around, in one form or another, since the early days of filmmaking. Sometimes they have been used for the "WOW" effect, sometimes to create a fantasy, and sometimes to move the story along. With the advent and enhancement of computer graphics and digitalization over the past twenty-five years, the use of these various visual effects has increased. For the purpose of this book, our discussion is limited to how to determine if they contribute to the underlying messages of a film, rather than how various effects are achieved.

In some earlier films, the grandeur and dominance of the special effects would grab the audience and be considered entertaining, but that was the extent of their success. The proper measure in film today is the success or lack of integration of the visual effects into the story. Their proper use should result in the effects becoming just another of the important elements of the film. Do they push the story forward or impede it? For example, in his May, 2004 review of *Van Helsing* in the *Sydney Morning Herald*, critic Paul Byrnes stated:

"It is beautifully shot, monumental in conception, full of amazing effects, and dull as someone else's tax returns. It is an example of everything that is wrong with Hollywood computer-generated-effects movies: technology swamps storytelling, action is rendered meaningless by exaggeration. . .."

The term special effects has evolved to include two distinct types of effects: those used on the set or mechanical effects and those created through CGI. The purpose of each, however, is the same—to create an on-screen image that would be too dangerous, too expensive, or perhaps simply impossible to achieve through other means.

Special effects are perceived by many as something spectacular. It is that perception that becomes an obstacle for the effects to serve a traditional narrative purpose. Viewers get sidetracked following the effects rather than immersing themselves into the story. At that point, the usage of effects has failed the director. But special effects can be used without viewers even realizing it and provide all sorts of "good." One example often cited is the filming of *Rabbit Proof Fence* (2002), a movie that used a number of child actors. If nighttime shots were required, a number of child labor laws would have kicked in. By using enhanced digital relighting of the some scenes shot during the day, to make them appear as if they were shot at night, the filming could progress, and the safety and welfare of the children was protected. The reality is that the spectacular effects comprise only a portion of the uses in mainstream movies.

One of the problems actors can face is performing when they cannot see the special effects because they are added digitally after the shooting. So they must imagine it and react as if it were right in front of them. A poor facial reaction or body language can destroy the scene in a flash. If the actor does not act as if he/she is really seeing the CGI and make us believe they see it, the audience will laugh or groan; the story will not be enhanced, and what follows no longer has impact.

There have been some excellent movies over the past fifteen years with some outstanding special effects. Think of *Inception* (2010), *Forest Gump* (1994), the *Harry Potter* series (2001–2011), *Avatar* (2009), *The Curious Case of Benjamin Button* (2008), *Lord of the Rings* (2002 and 2003), and other successful films. Unfortunately, there have been others that made a lot of noise, but left their story behind.

As I stated, in some cases, the special effects are specifically put in for the WOW effect, strictly entertainment rather than storytelling. This does not mean, however, that they should not have some direct relationship with the story. There is some evidence that appreciating special effects is age related, with younger viewers having the greater appreciation. But also remember that there are many films where the special effect usage is so well integrated that viewers do not realize the effects are present.

Visual Effects: Appreciating the Art

Think of the following when viewing films with special effects.

- See if you can identify when a special effect is being used.

- Then determine the director's purpose in using the effects and whether or not the usage fit into the film smoothly.

- Is there a successful integration of the visual effects into the story itself?

- Do the effects push the story forward or impede it?

- Decide if the message was effectively conveyed through the story, the effects, or an appropriately integrated mixture of both.

* * * * *

What follows is the story of how special effects were created and used in the film *The Curious Case of Benjamin Button* to assist in the storytelling and give it meaning. In this case the special effects were used to make the characters appear as people would during particular times of their lives.

THE CURIOUS CASE OF BENJAMIN BUTTON (2008)
- Directed by David Fincher
- Screenplay by Eric Roth based on the short story by F. Scott Fitzgerald
- Edited by Kirk Baxter and Angus Wall
- Distributed by Warner Brothers Paramount Pictures

For a complete list of the hundreds of people responsible for visual effects, special effects, and
art and make-up, be sure to see: *http://imdb.to/1RCty3r*

Primary Special-Effects Characters:
  Benjamin Button: Brad Pitt
  Daisy: Cate Blanchett

The story begins when a baby boy (Benjamin Button) is born with the appearance and physical maladies of an elderly man in his 80s. As he goes through life, he gradually grows younger. For example, seven years after he is born, Benjamin is seen in a wheelchair at a church with an old-time faith healer. He starts to walk and then is seen walking with a cane. As he becomes younger with age, the cane is discarded. He eventually meets Daisy as played by Elle Fanning, a seven-year-old granddaughter of one of the residents, and we watch the counter images: as Benjamin grows younger, Daisy grows older.

In the film, acting and special effects became interrelated. Neither Brad Pitt nor Cate Blanchett could have done the film without the movie's breakthrough technology, and the effects wouldn't have been the same without Pitt and Blanchett. To make the film, special-effects experts needed to put the head of an elderly Pitt on a child's body for the first third of the movie. The results look just like Pitt—only it isn't, of course. Similarly, when Blanchett's character does a dance scene in which a professional dancer doubles for her and when Daisy ages, a CGI head is used for her. The visual effects fit into the film smoothly. The film's message was conveyed through the integrated mixture of story and visual effect.

Steve Preeg, a character supervisor at Digital Domain, the studio that did all the special effects for the film, points out in a book on the making of the film that "[t]here's 325 shots—the first 52 minutes of the film—where there is no actual footage of Brad. He's not in any of the shots."[1] What the audience is actually seeing in the first third of the movie is a computer-generated copy of Pitt's head, which the studio aged digitally. The audience does, however, hear Pitt's voice throughout the film, until the end when a young child is used.

Visual effects supervisor, Eric Barba discusses the technology:

"We had to write code that covers every single lighting scenario and every single shot, a lighting system that mimics light on set. We also had to develop a system that would allow us to bring set lighting back into the CG world, the technique existed but the refinement of that technique had to be greater than ever before. We had to match the

---

1 David Fincher and Eric Roth, *The Curious Case of Benjamin Button: The making of the motion picture* (New York: Rizzoli International Publications, 2008), 128.

bounce of his step, the subtleties of color in the room, the reflections in the eyes, the movement of eyelashes and eyebrows, hair, teeth, gums and tongue. We had to make him a complete human being. That's the biggest challenge. After all the other biggest challenges, I mean." Pitt insisted that he did not want to only perform a portion of the movie. David Fincher told Barba, "Look, Benjamin has to be Brad. Brad has to drive the performance from beginning to end, so that there's a connection to him and the character. And that's the magic of it. It's Brad. It can't be another actor. Period."[2]

After creating a library of facial expressions and gestures while covered in a special substance, Pitt was filmed performing all of the scenes in the first third of the movie, and the special-effects gurus then mimicked his movements on the digital head. No makeup was used. One thing the process and the technology could not do, though, is understand the intent of the actor. Technology only sees a smile as a smile. It doesn't recognize an ironic smile, a happy smile, or a frustrated smile. Therefore, it took humans to push a scene one way or another.

Digital Domain's executive producer of visual effects, Ed Ulbrich, says Pitt made choices as an actor that no animator would have thought of doing. In the faith healer scene, "He ends up getting this kind of crazy kind of Popeye look on his face, and he's just thrilled. I don't think that it's

---

2 Ibid., 129.

something that any of us would have thought of had Brad not done that."[3]

At approximately fifty-two minutes in, Pitt begins to "age in reverse," and he wears less and less makeup until it's just Pitt. As he gets very young, there is digital touchup work on his physical makeup, then it is back to an even-younger digital head on his body—until, finally, several child actors and a baby were used at the end.

The old-looking baby used when Benjamin is born is a mixture of a live-action, radio-controlled model that was enhanced by visual effects company, Hydraulx. It has a rubber face and took three people to operate it. Eric Barba has explained that the first "digital-head" shot is the one where the audience sees Benjamin sitting at the table banging his spoon. That's the first body actor for Ben in his 80s. As he grows "younger," there is another body actor for him in his 70s, when he's on the tugboat with Cap'n Mike and then goes to the bar. One more body double was used for "Ben 60" when he leaves home. The body actors had different neck lengths and shoulder sizes. Even the arches of their necks were different, so a lot of massaging had to go on to make those heads feel like they belonged. One of the last "digital-head" shots is when Benjamin is reading the letter from Daisy on the back of the tugboat. The real Brad Pitt takes over at the point where he tells the captain, "Well you do drink a lot."

In an online interview for fxguide Eric Barba describes the overall process as including:

---

3 Ibid.

1. "Working from life-casts of Brad Pitt and body actors to create three photo-real maquettes [a handcrafted 3D model], representing Benjamin in his 80s, 70s, and 60s, then shooting them in different lighting conditions using a light stage.

2. Creating 3D computer scans of each of the three maquettes.

3. Shooting scenes on set with body actors in blue hoods.

4. Creating computer-based lighting to match the onset lighting for every frame in which Benjamin appears.

5. Having Brad perform facial expressions while being volumetrically captured, and creating a library of 'micro-expressions.'

6. Shooting Brad in high definition performing the role, from four camera angles, and using image analysis technology data to get animation curves and timings.

7. Matching the library of expressions to Brad's live performance of Benjamin.

8. Re-targeting the performance and expression data to the digital models of Benjamin (created

from scanning the maquettes) at the specific age required in the shot.

9. Finessing the performance to match current-Brad expressions to old-Benjamin physiology using hand animation.

10. Creating software systems for hair, eyes, skin, teeth, and all elements that make up Benjamin.

11. Creating software to track the exact movements of the body actor and the camera, to integrate the CG head precisely with the body.

12. Compositing all of Benjamin's elements to integrate animation, lighting, and create the final shot."[4]

Other special effects of note in the film include:

a. In a scene somewhat early in the film, one of the residents of the old-age home where Benjamin is being raised is trying to teach him how to play the piano. Neither the extra nor Pitt could play, so hand doubles had to be used for both of them. In other words, viewers saw the two actors sitting at the piano but other people's hands playing were

---

4 "The Curious Case of Aging Visual Effects," an interview of Eric Barba conducted by Mike Seymour on January 1, 2009. http://www.fxguide.com/featured/The_Curious_Case_of_Aging_Visual_Effects/.

edited into the shot. The color of the skin had to keep changing to match the rest of the scene.

b. Fooling with the patina of the film with light flashes and scratches, for the early scenes involving the Gateau family, to make it seem as if the film was from 1918.

c. When Benjamin goes out with Mr. Odi and rides the streetcar, the scene had to be shot with a blue-screen background and then digitally placed into a streetcar because the scene was shot shortly after hurricane Katrina, and the streetcars were not yet running.

Once the various special effects were edited into a scene, the film editor then had to provide the continuity and make the appropriate cuts and dissolves so they looked realistic. The statistical information on the film states that over 150 people were involved in the design, creation, and use of the special effects alone.

Go to *http://digitaldomain.com/work/the-curious-case-of-benjamin-button/* for a video showing how Digital Domain accomplished much of the above.

CHAPTER SEVEN

Sound and Music

When most moviegoers think about the beginnings of sound in movies, they talk of *The Jazz Singer* (1927), which was the first talkie. The fact is, however, that films had sound almost from the beginning. Silent films were usually accompanied by live music and, at times, even sound effects. In larger venues, this was provided by orchestras in the pit. In smaller theaters, there was a piano or organ player providing the sound. Studios often provided full orchestral arrangements along with the reels of film. Today, digital soundtracks are added to most films, often providing a full 360° surround-sound experience.

There are three forms of cinematic sound: speech, music, and sound effects. Sometimes one is used to imitate or create the effect of another. Purists would argue that silence is another form of cinematic sound. Most sounds are mixed in a studio, not done on the set. *Sound mixing*, which is the selection and combining of sounds, is the job of the sound editor. He/she chooses the sounds based on what the director wants the mood and the emphasis or background in a scene to be. Just like everyday life, there is usually a combination of sounds. Because we have learned to ignore many of the environmental sounds we encounter in our everyday lives, sound becomes a very difficult technique to use in film.

Münsterberg's six elements are just as much at play with the use of sound, if not more so, as they are with images. Russian filmmaker Sergei Eisenstein likened the adding of sound to images as "the synchronisation of the senses." Pitch, volume, tone, reverberation, and tempo of the sounds affect the viewer's attention, responses, and comprehension. High-pitched sounds might convey suspense or fear, while low-pitched ones could convey calm or seriousness. Sounds have rhythms that may or may not match the rhythm of the images—with each combination resulting in a different effect.

> "Sound is fifty percent of the motion picture experience, and I've always believed audiences are moved and excited by what they hear in my movies, at least as much as by what they see."
> —George Lucas, director, screenwriter, and industry innovator

There are two types of sounds found in a film, regardless of the form, and either may occur on-screen or off-screen.

1. Sound that characters can hear.

    a. This may have a physical source in the film (called *external diegetic*), or

    b. it may come solely from inside the character's mind, which is termed *internal diegetic*.

2.   Sound that a character cannot hear (non-diegetic).

Off-screen sound creates an illusion of bigger space. It can also fill in the details to complete some images in our minds. While critical to the film's experience, leaving it up to the viewer's imagination to fill in the missing image saves directors both time and money.

Sound waves create vibrations that affect the viewer/listener in not only a sensory manner but also physically. The vibrations hitting the body cause a visceral reaction. Sounds may be pleasing, exciting, soothing, or irritating. The sounds associated with an image increase the depth and intensity of our experience.

Meaning and emotion can be expressed not only through dialogue but also by using certain music and sound effects. Absolute silence can call attention and convey an emotion or meaning. In *Amour*, discussed later in this book, the actors frequently convey strong messages through their eyes and facial expressions without a word being spoken. If there is a loud, fast-paced sound in the background of a film that suddenly stops and there is silence, the impression of death or trouble is created.

With the exception of dialogue, most moviegoers consider sound an accompaniment. It can, however, be the sole thing that provides meaning to an image. A number of experiments have been conducted showing viewers the same image a number of times, but each time the accompanying sound is changed. Each sound change resulted in a totally different response and interpretation from the viewers.

"In motion pictures both image and sound must be treated with special care. In my view, a motion picture stands or falls on the effective combination of these two factors. Truly cinematic sound is neither merely accompanying sound (easy and explanatory) nor the natural sounds captured at the time of the simultaneous recording. In other words, cinematic sound is that which does not simply add to, but multiplies, two or three times, the effect of the image."

—Akira Kurosawa, director

Sound editing is just as exacting as editing the images. The use of a particular sound guides the attention to and perception of the image by the viewer. Sounds may carry over from one scene to another as a transition mechanism. A sound may keep recurring throughout the film as a way of tying scenes together. Just like the other cinematic elements, sounds can be hard or soft, up close or far, clear or muffled, constant or staccato. Each variation and combination thereof affects the viewer's response and the meaning drawn.

Foreign-language films present other sound problems if the viewer does not understand the language. Because of the timing some sounds may seem out of place. Some films are dubbed in English. Obviously the lips and the sounds don't match and are rarely in sync. The inflections are also often misleading. Many people have trouble keeping up with English subtitles, so they lose a lot of meaning. A trick to use is to keep the sound on so that you hear the inflections and rhythm of the foreign dialogue while reading the subtitles. In some languages even this does not help, unfortunately, because the cadence doesn't flow.

In the introduction, I spoke of letting yourself "open up" to the vibes coming at you from the screen and speakers. To now expand on that thought, I suggest that to fully appreciate a film, one must not only see each image but be prepared to both hear and listen to the sounds of the film. Filmgoers often *hear* music playing in the background yet rarely *listen* to exactly what it is or to the words. Sometimes, there are important hints to be taken from these elements, other times the words tell the story. Examples coming immediately to mind are "Smoke Gets in Your Eyes" in *45 Years* (2015), "Imagine" in *The Killing Fields* (1990), "Lilac Love" in *Tell No One* (2006)

* * * * *

Ask ten people coming out of a movie what they thought of the music and the effect it had on the story and them. In most cases, at least seven of them will not be able to answer you. Although it was there, the music didn't register consciously, but rest assured it had an impact. Noted film composer David Raskin believes that film music best performs its role without an intervening conscious act of perception. That is, when the music and/or words register with us in a way that we do not realize it's actually happening. One of the keys will be whether or not the music is heard by the characters in the film or if it is off-screen and in the background.

Generally, only one-third of a film contains music, yet it plays an extremely important role in a film. For instance, it can:

- establish time, place, and ethnicity through identifiable rhythms; music establishes locale or historical periods;

- establish a certain tone and or mood;

- help to signify an event or provide a symbolic meaning;

- be an aural extension of the visual by helping to convey the thoughts or emotions of the characters or situation; music then becomes a psychological force upon the viewer;

- build suspense;

- be heard by the characters as part of the scene;

- link or transition scenes; and

- provide "theme music" for opening or ending of film.

Just as light affects the metabolism, so too does music affect the viewer's state of being. Sometimes music can help to identify a time period either by the type of music used or a song the audience is bound to remember. In *Dr. Strangelove*

(1964), starting with the opening scene and throughout the movie, a number of easily recognizable musical pieces are heard for comedic or satiric effect. Sometimes music is used to fill the absence of dialogue. Action scenes, such as fights, wars, and long marches, and adventure films with giant rolling rocks coming at the characters, are examples of such.

Like dialogue and the camera, music can also convey a point of view. Early Russian filmmakers insisted that music should not simply be an accompaniment, it should be an integral part of the scene. Yet, musical accompaniment can add qualities to a character or identify the character. It must be used carefully and inserted at the appropriate moments, even if those moments only last seconds. Many directors try to find music they believe the character would like or listen to in the life portrayed. On the supplemental disc accompanying *The Truman Show* DVD (2005), director Peter Weir offered the following insight:

"When making a film, I play music constantly during "dailies" – the nightly screenings of the previous day's shooting. I test all kinds of music against the image, searching for the elusive 'sound' of the picture. In the case of *The Truman Show*, since it is the story of a live television program, I also was determining the music that the show's creator, Christof, would have chosen. The tracks that seemed to be drawing the most out of the images for me were those of Philip Glass."

Weir also used a score by Burkhard Dallwitz to go along with those tracks: ". . .and from the moment he played back his first cue, I know Christof would have been as delighted with the result as I was."

The jazz in *Good Night and Good Luck* (2005) acts as a transition tool and the lyrics tell what is coming up. The music heard in Spike Lee's *Do the Right Thing* (1989) has an almost dissonant effect. The loud, active, vibrant beat of soul and rap does work well against the melodious jazz jams. The music helps convey the various tensions in very different worlds of the cultures even though they exist in the same neighborhood.

Compare that with the steady constant theme of the music in *The Big Chill* (1983). Its music is all rock recordings popular when the characters were in college together—ten years before the time in which the movie is set. The director's wife put together a collection of music that she and her husband enjoyed when they were in school. With a couple of exceptions, the actors did not hear the music; in fact, they did not even know what song was being played. All they knew was that they had to speak loudly because they were supposed to be talking over the music. In a dinner scene where everyone ends up dancing, the cast was told the song. They tried doing the scene with the melody in their minds, but ended up having to get wireless earpieces to listen to the real song as they acted and danced.

In another scene, two actors driving in an open jeep had to pretend they had the radio on and were moving to the beat and tapping the steering wheel or dashboard. This time they had to do it without the benefit of hearing the music. The film editor, Carol Littleton, said she looked for what worked best rhythmically and dramatically. The film's director, Lawrence Kasdan, chose the music for each scene to enhance the drama without directly commenting on what was taking place in each scene.

Music can fill in the gaps in the viewer's imagination by suggesting hidden emotions or off-screen action. It can hint at what is to come or an unidentified location, or it may lead the viewer's imagination down a particular path. Linking certain characters with particular music helps convey the type of person they are. Have you ever noticed when hearing a particular song you instantly think of a certain movie, even though the song was an independent hit?

The following is an excerpt from *John Williams's Film Music* section entitled *What Does a Shark Sound Like?*[1] explaining how the music was used in *Jaws:*

"Unlike the "weird melody" in line with the tradition of horror music that Spielberg expected-dissonant and harmonically eerie, as the more tonal passages of the score for Images are-Williams opted for a closer musical equivalent of the shark, a primitive pulsation with no melody at all. Indeed, melody is a product of artistic civilization, which by its nature brings traces of history and culture:

> "I fiddled around with the idea of creating something
> that was very . . . brainless, . . . like the shark. All
> instinct . . . Meaning something [that] could be
> very repetitious, very visceral, and grab you in your
> gut, not in your brain. Remember, Steven didn't

1 Emilio Audissinoi, *John Williams's Film Music* (Wisconsin: University of Wisconsin Press, 2014), 111 - 114

have the computer shark. He only had his rubber ducky, so the simple idea of that bass ostinato, just repeating those two notes and introduce a third note when you don't expect it and so on. It could be something you could play very softly, which would indicate that the shark is far away when all you see is water. Brainless music that gets louder and gets closer to you, something is gonna swallow you up."[2]

Williams came up with the primitive rhythmic simplicity of an ostinato, that is, a brief repeating and hammering fragment, more rhythmic than melodic.

Those three repeated bass notes recall the heartbeat, the primordial rhythm of life. Their seemingly unstoppable constant and mechanical repetition effectively represents the shark: a primitive yet proficient killing machine, moved only by the instinct for eating.

In addition to characterizing the nature of the monster, the shark's motif performs another important function within the film, a function that Spielberg's "weird melody" could hardly have carried out. Being an ostinato, the shark motif can be more easily shortened, prolonged, or repeated in loops as required by visuals, so to become the aural equivalent of the shark's movement through space. Williams commented, "I thought that altering the speed and volume of the theme, from very slow to very fast, from very soft to very loud, would indicate the mindless attacks of the shark. Steven was a bit skeptical, but when

---

2 Rebecca Keegan, *John Williams and Steven Spielberg Mark 40 Years of Collaboration.* (Los Angeles Times, Jan. 8, 2012)

the orchestra performed the piece, it worked better than we had anticipated."[3] Music is often the only sign of the presence of the monster that can be perceived, since the monster itself is off-screen for most of the time. Williams plays fair with the audience, since the shark motif is not used to cheat when the shark is not around but is played only when it is present. For example, in the fake-fin prank scene, visually we can be led to take it as a real fin, but there is no music accompanying it, thus signaling that the shark is not there. On the contrary, in the same sequence, the music anticipates the real shark being spotted in the estuary. The shark's motif does not just perform the function of classical leitmotiv but is also a peculiar type of Mickey-Mousing: the music adheres perfectly to the spatial movements of the beast. But, unlike the classical Mickey-Mousing that replicated the on-screen movements, in this case it mostly indicates off-screen movements.

Consider Chrissie's death scene at the beginning of the film: it is the music that conveys the "obscene" violence and horror of the underwater off-screen attack - obsene being Latin for "off-stage." Chrissie undresses and decides to take a nude night swim in the sea. A point-of-view shot looking up from the abyss shows us the body of the girl on the surface-as in the opening titles, we are seeing through the eyes of a mysterious sea creature. We hear a harp arpeggio evoking the waves, then two of those ominous low notes, which we have previously identified with the sea creature. The notes become louder and repeat faster and faster as the

3 Laurent Bouzereau, *Jaws*, CD Booklet (Decca 2000, 467 045-2)8-10

creature approaches the girl and points at its prey. Then, the narration reverses the perspective and cuts to Chrissie on the sea surface. Suddenly, something we cannot see starts pulling her down: the action is marked with a violently iforzando horns rip, a kind of rrrrrruhah! That is the shark's bite; the music conveys both the shark's fury and Chrissie's pain. She screams while she is tossed around. We do not see what is happening beneath the surface, but we can easily imagine the horrible scene of the shark tearing its victim. Frantic shrill violin writing, violent percussion, and repeated horns "bites" depict the off-screen violence. The scene takes shape in our imagination through music, which fulfills both a spatial perceptive and an emotive function.

The shark motif replicates the shark's movements on both the horizontal and the vertical axes. Horizontal trajectories are rendered through variations of dynamics and tempo: when the music slows down and the volume decreases, we know that the shark is slowing its pace; when the music speeds up or the volume increases we know that the shark is attacking. Movements on the vertical axis are rendered through variations of orchestral texture: when the writing gets thicker, we know that the shark is coming to the surface; when the writing thins down to dark timbres only (contrabasses, cellos, bassoons) we know that the beast is plunging into the dark abyss. For example, consider the pier scene in which two islanders try to hook the shark, with the only result of having the pier torn away, falling into the water, and thus risking being eaten up. When the shark bites the bait and points offshore, dragging along the torn pier to which the bait was fastened, the shark ostinato starts, played by contrabasses and cellos. The ostinato keeps playing at the same level and speed during the tearing off of the pier and the falling into the water of the two men, one of which is pulled offshore along with the pier. At one point, the pier stops and suddenly reverses, indicating that the shark is now pointing to the swimming islander. Violins and violas abruptly join the cellos and contrabasses in playing the ostinato, followed by the horns menacingly presenting the second shark motif. The music's speed and volume increase as the shark chases the man who is frantically trying to reach the shore and come out of the water. The man succeeds, and the shark has to retreat. The music deflates, gradually decelerating and turning into a single sustained bass note that closes the scene.

Another function of the score is to further separate the two worlds-the shark below and the humans above-and this is accomplished by using the timbres of the orchestra. The monster shark lives down, below the water surface; humans live above the surface. The difference between the humans' world - lit by the sun-and the shark's world-the abyss in which darkness reigns - is marked by the contrast between the shark music- mechanical, low pitched, with dark timbre - and the human music-melodic, higher pitched, and with the bright timbres of violins, flutes, and trumpets.

The *Jaws* score has the important emotive function of creating suspense, anxiety, fear. Yet its most successful contribution consists in its embodying the shark and skillfully tracing its movements both on-screen and off-screen. The score is particularly outstanding for its spatial perceptive function."

Music is the communicating "vibe" from the screen to the audience that envelops them and helps to create a single experience. Now that my fellow film-group members have learned to listen for the music whenever it appears, they find their film enjoyment greatly enhanced. They are quick to tell me about how beautiful, or stirring, or dramatic it was. When Aristotle insisted that rhythm was a required element of drama, he was talking about the "music" of the chorus in ancient tragedies. The only thing that has changed in filmmaking is the format. Like every other element we have discussed, music is an integral part of a film's story and its message. Music provides for a visceral reaction and gets or directs our attention.

Sound and Music: Appreciating the Art

When evaluating how sound and music are working in a film, ask yourself the following questions:

- Are the sounds directing your attention?

- Are you getting a visceral or an emotional reaction caused by the sound?

- Does the music match the natural rhythms of the film?

- Does the music have a specific purpose or is it just in the background?

- Is the music part of the story?

- Does the music affect you emotionally?

- If the score was removed would you realize it?

EXAMPLES OF EFFECTIVE MUSIC USE

MOVIE	*MUSIC*	*WHY*
Jaws Steven Speilberg Music/John Williams	John Williams' simple two note ostinato bass pattern boosted the composer into additional stardom coming on the heels of his previous scores for "star wars". In combination with Steven Speilberg's visuals the movie vaulted into stardom.	Thematic bass pattern (EF,EF,EF) varied in intensity, speed, produced a leitmotif which became one of filmdom's most recognized two note identities – a shark.
The Birds Alfred Hitchcock Music Coordination By Bernard Hermann	The movie contained no incidental score music. The sound effect created for the birds becomes the significant thematic material in the movie in counterpoint to silence to create the psychological effects. Bernard Hermann is "musical consultant". Incidental music by Claude Debussy	A special sound machine which mimics pigeons sound is used as the basis for identifying fear, impending or immediate danger unlike the jaws theme which is a musical representation of similar scenes.
Catch Me If You Can Steven Speilberg Music/John Williams	John William's score illustrates a total departure for the composer from his regular and usual lyrical, rhythmic and more traditional approach to movie music. William's roots are embedded in the jazz of the 60's, 70's and 80's and this is illustrated by a jazz score rich in jazz heritage and instrumentation.	William's use of traditional jazz instruments (lead sax, woodwind section, brass lines and rhythm) are significant in the sound of the movie. In addition, the music not only replicates the music of the era, but also has a mystery feel in the use of melodic character and hesitating rhythms. A truly unique score for Williams.

Casablanca Michael Curtiz Music/Max Steiner	"As Time Goes By" becomes the bedrock of the movie's theme and identifies strongly with the star Humphrey Bogart/music by Max Steiner	The song "As Time Goes By" is used in many forms (major key/minor key/as a waltz/as a fox trot) to illustrate the film's various emotions
Titanic James Cameron Music/James Horner	James Horner's score was everything Cameron had desired. It jumps from intimacy to huge grand scenes and deftly navigates happiness and sadness. 75% of the score was synthesizer and voice with wordless vocals (Norwegian star Sissle Kyrkjebo) and the remaining being the full orchestra and chorus.	Horner's main use of the synthesizer is to create organic colors. Thus, he uses a layered effect with various tones in combinations. Horner wrote four basic themes which are used throughout the 138 minutes of scored music. It is this use of "painting" the scenes with colors that makes this score so meaningful along with, of course, the title song which became a large hit and moneymaker on its own.
Gladiator Ridley Scott Music/Hans Zimmer & Lee Gerrard	Hans Zimmer (who does not know a note of music and, thus, relies on the use of electronic keyboards, etc.) In tandem with singer Lee Gerrard has composed a martial and ethereal score a step up from the traditional great epics of "ten commandments", "Spartacus" and others. Although Zimmer uses a great deal of computer technology and electronic sound in the score it does not sound like it. This is because they are muted and fit in with the overall score and the special vocal effects of Gerrard. Zimmer first gained attention with his score to "Rain Man"	Zimmer collaborates with singer Lee Gerrard and producing a score combining orchestra, electronics, and the human voice. On the thematic side there are 19 distinct themes in the movie. It took Zimmer and Gerrard more than six months to write the score. An eternity in movie land. However, given the time, both composers have almost created an opera. The use of chorus and Gerrard's voice add such a romantic and emotional feel to the movie that it attracted many female viewers. That was part of Zimmer's desire.

CHAPTER EIGHT

Acting

While numerous elements, such as special effects, lighting, sound, and music—for example—help enhance a viewer's perception of a character, it is the actor's portrayal that gives a script's character an existence, a personality, a meaning. Often when film-group members say they don't like an actor's performance, I ask them to first determine if what they saw was an actor doing his or her best with a bad script *or* an actor failing to get into the character and making it real. Sometimes, obviously, it can be a little of both. Then there are those situations in which the actor is, in reality, doing a wonderful job of making you feel a character's shallowness, which is much harder than creating a strong character.

Each character in a film is a combination of three visions: The first vision is the writer's. Then there is the interpretive vision of the actor, and lastly there is the interpretive message of the director. Many actors use a set of techniques to help them create what they perceive to be a realistic portrayal. These techniques are known as the Stanislavski method (named after Russian actor Constantin Stanislavski, who developed the method in 1916). The goal is for the actors to have a deep understanding of the motivation, objectives, and obstacles of a character in each moment of time depicted. To help the actor connect to the character, Stanislavski suggested that the actors constantly ask themselves, "What if this situation happened to me?" By using the identical processes Münsterberg held that viewers must use (perception, attention, memory, imagination, suggestion, and emotions), actors develop their characters.

"Method acting," which was developed by American actor and director Lee Strasberg, carries the Stanislavski method even further by calling for the actors to become completely immersed in the characters they are playing at all times. There are many stories of actors who, once the shooting began, never got out of a character for a single second: offstage, off the set, at home, wherever.

Utilizing this concept, Lawrence Kasdan, the director of *The Big Chill* (1983), required the ensemble cast to live in the same condominium building during the film's entire shoot. He also had the entire cast on the set every day, even if they were not in the scenes being shot. This was unheard of since actors always went back to their dressing rooms between their shots or stayed home if they were not in any shots that day. Kasdan wanted his cast to build the personal closeness and camaraderie their characters enjoyed in the movie.

No matter which acting method is used, it is not enough to rely on what is written on the page. The actor and the director must gain a deeper understanding by internally asking some questions to help them get to know the character better and give a more believable performance. They must fill in the spaces about the character's life.

"A film actor must be able to dream another person's dreams before he can call that character his own. Film acting was never easy but during the past fifty years, the craft has become even more demanding, partly because of changes in technology, partly because of the increased requirements actors and directors have placed upon themselves, and partly because of shifts in audience expectations."
—Michael Caine, actor

Actor and director John Cassavetes relates the story of going to his father to say, "I don't want to go to college. I want to be an actor." Cassavetes continues, "He gave me this very solemn look and I thought: *Oh, my God, I'm really gonna get it*. And [his father] said 'Well, that's a very noble thing to do, but do you know what kind of responsibility that is? You are going to have to be truthful to each of those characters' human nature.'"[1]

From time to time, the actor and director will differ on how a role should be played. Knowing when to yield to the actor's view is one of the traits of a good director. In *Do the Right Thing* (1989), writer and director Spike Lee strongly believed the white pizzeria owner, Sal, was a racist. The actor playing this role, Danny Aiello, disagreed just as strongly. The result was a moderated portrayal that was dominated by Aiello's viewpoint. Another well-known battle, related by

---

1 John Cassavetes, *Cassavetes on Cassavetes*, edited by Ray Carney (London: Faber & Faber, 2001).

James Cameron about *Aliens* (1986), was his disagreement with Sigourney Weaver, who once again played the heroine Ripley in the sequel, over the character's complex feelings about the alien. Weaver refused to "hate" the alien and played the role accordingly.

If while watching a film you perceive someone is "acting," then that actor has failed to make the character real or believable. When you know you are watching the *actor* and not the *character*, then the illusion is gone, possibly along with the actor's career. When an actor's portrayal does not seem to meld with the other characters or fit into the overall scheme of the screenplay, then the actor's vision of the role is wrong. One might say the director also failed by allowing a poor performance.

In accepting the Best Supporting Actor award at the 2015 Screen Actors Guild Awards, actor J. K. Simmons pointed out that, whether the actor is in every shot or only has one line, "All of us actors are supporting actors. Each of us is not only supporting the story, the movie, the play or whatever we are doing. Each of us is essential, completely crucial to the story because if there is one false movement, that train comes off the rails and our suspension of disbelief is gone and we have to bring it back."

Audiences have become more movie savvy and, accordingly, their expectations affect actors' portrayals. Audiences expect a realistic performance, something that *appears* to be true. Some of this can be conveyed through body language, and the subtlest movement can make a scene. A character's facial expression, vocal inflection, posture are just some of the human traits that express feelings. Perhaps one of the most classical examples of expression is found in Ingrid Bergman's performance in *Casablanca* (1942). Her natural ability to demurely look down while sitting and talking with Humphrey Bogart conveys so much more emotion in her scenes than any dialogue could. Six-time Academy Award-nominated Glenn Close has said that after watching her own performance in *The Big Chill* (1983), which was only her second film, she realized that "[t]houghts are powerful on camera." Words are not always necessary to convey the message.

The actor's job seems even harder when one realizes that the vast majority of movies are shot out of sequence. The director does not begin shooting the first scenes and go straight through to the end, as in a play. Rather, all shots taking place in one location, regardless of *when* they occur in the movie, are shot together. Another example of shooting out of sequence comes when two or more actors are engaged in a scene. First the "master shot," one showing everyone, is filmed, in which the actors run through the entire scene. Then the medium shots and finally the close-ups are shot. An actor will be asked to go through all of the dialogue that occurs from a particular spot and angle regardless of when it actually occurs. Editing then cuts and pastes frames into the right order.

Many so-called prima-donna actors leave their co-actors alone during this sequence, requiring them to carry on a conversation with an imaginary person or a script person reading the lines with no affect. One classic scene in which this occurred is the taxicab scene in *On The Waterfront* (1954), where the two brothers (played by Marlon Brando and Rod

Steiger) have a strong difference of opinion. After the joint set-up shots, Steiger had to deliver his lines in the close-ups with the script manager, because Brando just left the set. Steiger never forgave Brando for that insult.[2]

Another time this occurred was in *Mo' Better Blues* (1990) during the shooting of the dream love scene between Bleek (played by Denzel Washington) and his two girlfriends (played by Joie Lee and Cynda Williams). Washington stayed around for his close-ups and then left. The two women, both topless for the scene, helped each other by reading Bleek's lines for the other's shots. This was certainly better than having a script girl do it, for at least the actors were in the scene and felt it and understood.[3]

The mark of the greatest actors is their innate ability to take on numerous quite different characters and play each with absolutely strong, believable performances. In this regard Meryl Streep is considered by many to be the greatest actor of all time. Consider just these few examples over the short period of 5 years.

- Miranda Priestly –Demanding editor of a high fashion magazine (*The Devil Wears Prada* - 2006)

- Sister Aloysius Beauvier- Catholic school principal questioning a priest's relationship with a male student. (*Doubt*-2008)

---

2 Rod Steiger – Scene By Scene (BBC) 2000

3 Spike Lee with Lisa Jones, *Mo' Better Blues* (Fireside Book, New York 1990)

- Julia Childs – Famous chef – (*Julie and Julia* 2009)

- Margaret Thatcher – Former British Prime Minister (*The Iron Lady* – 2011)

Ms. Streep was nominated for over 300 awards for these portrayals, winning many.

Acting: Appreciating the Art

Ask yourself the following questions about a film's actors:

- Were the actors believable in their roles?

- Were you able to forget who the actor was and concentrate on the character?

- If you did not like the performance was it because the actor didn't belong in that role, or was the acting inferior or the role poorly written?

- Did the actor "become" the character on screen?

- Did the actors enhance each other's performances, and did they play off each other well?

- Did any of the supporting actors particularly stand out?

- Did the director place the camera in the right position for you to see and appreciate the characters?

PART THREE

The Filmmakers
and Their Techniques

CHAPTER NINE

The Director

As discussed earlier, there are many people and departments responsible for making a movie. There are three people, however, who have the most influence on what the audience will see: the director, the cinematographer (sometimes billed as the director of photography), and the film editor. Consider them the "Board of Directors" of a film, so to speak.

In the course of making a film, the entire triumvirate of director, cinematographer, and film editor will get to know how each other think; what they like or don't like; and how they want to convey a film's message, along with numerous other preferences—but the director is ultimately in charge. The key, obviously, is comfort, trust, and compatible visions. When the same team works together often, there is an even better chance that their films will take on an auteur appearance and feel. This gives rise to the question of whether auteur refers to single authorship (i.e., the director) or multiple authorship composed of the entire team.

Technically, a film's story begins with the screenwriter. However, if the movie is adapted from another work, one could say the film's story begins with the author, although it is rare for any film to stay 100% true to the original work; the screenwriter and the director usually edit and rewrite the original story to fit into a cinematic environment. Then the director decides which parts of the story to emphasize and also adds some additional scripting to enhance the meaning(s) he or she wishes to convey. Most directors want to tell a particular story and seek the best vehicle to achieve their goal.

A recent example is the 2014 production of *Selma*. The focus of the film is the famous march from Selma to Montgomery, Alabama, led by Dr. Martin Luther King, Jr., which was an historic moment in the civil-rights struggle. The director, Ava DuVernay, has said that the original screenplay needed extensive reworking because it was a "traditional biopic" that adhered to antiquated and patronizing ideas about history and the civil-rights movement. DuVernay told the *Boston Globe*: "We've grown up as a country and cinema should be able to reflect what's true. And what's true is that black people are the center of their own lives and should tell their own stories from their own perspectives."

The ensuing controversy surrounding the film centered on how DuVernay chose to portray what happened between Dr. King and President Lyndon Johnson. She admitted that some artistic license was taken (not an unusual occurrence), but insisted that the revisionism was necessary for the movie. President Johnson's supporters, on the other hand, believed the movie went too far in its misrepresentation of the facts. When marketing the film, DuVernay made it clear that the film was *not* meant to be a biopic, but rather a dramatic representation of the people and the time.

Dr. King's speeches in the film are not exact because Dr. King's estate would not give the producers a reasonable licensing rate for them, so all of the speeches used in the movie were written to convey Dr. King's messages without quoting him. In these instances, is the filmmaker responsible for taking additional steps to ensure that no viewer believes the film is a 100% accurate representation of historical events? Many films today begin with the admonition: "Based on a true event." Others avoid that because they believe it casts the entire film into a purely fictional light.

One of the first things a viewer needs to consider when analyzing a film is the time/era in which the movie was made *and* the time period depicted in the film. What was going on in the world at that time depicted that relates to the story being told? Sometimes, meanings conveyed are obvious, but other times they can be subtle. Often, a director does not even realize the meaning or implications they have inserted into a scene. These come from the director's own culture and life experiences and are so much a part of the person that they fail to recognize the message conveyed. Likewise, the viewer may perceive a meaning from a scene that was never intended by the filmmaker. This perception comes from the viewer's life experiences or culture.

To paraphrase director Lindsay Anderson: a film is created under the director's guidance and then transformed from the inadequately expressed idea of the script to a living personification through sound and images. Anderson believed that the camera's images are the chief means of expression in the cinema. Such a view is at odds with those who say the actors fill that role. Agreeing with Anderson, writer/director David Mamet gets a little more specific, saying that he provides "a succession of images juxtaposed so that the contrast between these images moves the story forward in the mind of the audience."[1]

There is also a very small group of original, idiosyncratic directors who use offbeat methods to develop their films. In presenting British Director Mike Leigh with the 2015 British Academy of Film and Television Arts (BAFTA) Fellowship Award (the organization's highest honor), actress Imelda Staunton described his method as follows: "He has devised and directed twenty feature films, all starting without a script. He and his actors create and develop characters which he then shapes into his stories. . . . He deals with the very essence of who we are and what we feel. He shows how extraordinary, ordinary life can be."

The next day, an article appeared in *The Guardian* newspaper in England reporting on some comments made about director Terrence Malick (*Days of Heaven*, *The Thin Red Line*, *Tree of Life*) from two actors in his films:

> "Christian Bale has admitted he was left a little clueless as to what was going on during the making of Terrence Malick's latest film. Speaking over the weekend at the Berlin film festival...Bale said he shot his part without a script and did not receive any instruction from the maverick film-maker to help him paint a picture of the movie's theme. 'He didn't tell us what it was about,' Bale said. 'He really just

---

1 David Mamet, On Directing Film (New York: Penguin Books, 1992), 2.

gave me the character description. We worked on
the character a great deal, worked on his backstory.

"He added: 'I never had any lines to learn, but I'd see
other people, and they'd have pages. I'd always look
over their shoulders to see what it was that I was
going to be told. I never knew what I was going to
be doing each day.' The double Oscar-winning actor
also revealed Malick's penchant for 'torpedoing' his
cast with 'different actors and nonactors to get a
very real response.'" [2]

Director John Sayles has revealed using a similar technique
to that described by Bale: If he is shooting many takes of a
scene with more than one actor and he sees one of them
slowing down, in one of the takes, he instructs the other
actor to change his/her answer during the dialogue in order
to keep the opposing actor fresh. This obviously does not
torpedo a scene, but rather helps bring out the best from
the actor.

Often, film critics and academicians offer their analyses
of what the director and/or actor were trying to accomplish
or whose style was being imitated. But in reality, the one
process that defies such opinions is the uniqueness of the
artist. It is the artist's personal perception, abilities, decisions,
and choices that define the work. While a director or actor
may sometimes pay homage to a prior work, the fact that
a film critic interprets the style as one associated with an
earlier filmmaker does not mean the current artist was even

2 Christian Bale was baffled by Terrence Malick on Knight of Cups shoot, *The
Guardian*, February 9, 2015

aware of the style or if it influenced them. It is often just a case of the critics applying an intellectualization based upon their own personal movie experiences.

The noted Swedish director Ingmar Bergman described his art: "To make a film is for me a very personal experience. It is a driving force like hunger and thirst. Some people express themselves by writing books, painting pictures, climbing mountains, beating their children or dancing the samba. I express myself by making films."[3]

Just like the brushstrokes of a painter, the director, through the use of camera placement, light and shadow, can present subject matter anyway he wishes it to be perceived by the viewer. As author Lewis Jacobs has observed, "Skillfully used light and shade – through designed chiaroscuro and the degrees of brightness, darkness, diffusion and intensity of illumination–are an effective means for evoking atmosphere, form, mood, and emotion, endowing the pictorial image with clarity, vigor and design."[4]

Agreeing with Rob Reiner, director David Fincher (*The Social Network, Gone Girl, Curious Case of Benjamin Button*) claims that his responsibility is to "place your eye where I think is best. It is a psychology of a cinematic moment. Where am I taking your eye? What did you need to know?. . ..You have control of everything that the audience sees and hears for two hours and they know it. . .. Every time you go to a close-up the audience knows it is important. But

---

3 Ingmar Bergman, "Self Analysis of a Filmmaker" essay in *The Ingmar Bergman Archives*, edited by Paul Duncan and Bengt Wanselius (Cologne, Germany: Tashen America, 2008).

4 Lewis Jacobs, The Movies As Medium (New York: Octagon Books, 1973), 24.

is it real or a red herring that you will reveal later in the movie?" [5]

Whether an auteur or a first timer, directors stress the necessity of collaboration with a number or people in filmmaking, including producers, screenwriters, actors, cinematographers, editors, and composers or music directors. Bernardo Bertolucci described his directing maturation thus: "In my mind, I made a film alone: I was its auteur in the strictest sense. Then, with time, I realized that a director can express his fantasies even better if he is able to stimulate the creativity of everyone around him. A film is sort of a melting pot in which the talents of a crew must mingle."[6]

Pedro Almodóvar explains why: "You can choose the frame, but when it comes to shooting, everything is in the hands of the camera operator. You can talk for hours and hours about the light you want, but in the end, only the gaffer decides what the light will be like. And it doesn't matter . . ..because there are areas in which your control remains complete–areas that you must concentrate on. . .the text; the actors performance; and the choice of the main color, the one that will dominate in the sets, costumes, and the film's general tone."[7]

5 David Fincher, "Film School Through Commentaries–David Fincher," www. filmschoolthrucommentaries.wordpress.com.

6 Laurent Tirard, ed., "Interview with Bernardo Bertolucci," *Moviemakers' Master Class: Private Lessons from the World's Foremost Directors* (New York: Faber and Faber, 2002), 50.

7 Laurent Tirard, ed., "Interview with Pedro Almodóvar," *Moviemakers' Master Class: Private Lessons from the World's Foremost Directors* (New York: Faber and Faber, 2002), 85.

Although many directors have a special cinematographer in whom they place extreme trust, and the two know each other so well they blend to one vision, most directors still list the ability to work well with the actors as the key to successful filmmaking. Some directors allow the actors a good deal of freedom to develop their roles as they see and feel them. Some allow full improvisation. Director Robert Altman allowed extensive improvisation, while Robert Wise relied on preproduction planning and storyboarded entire films. However, Wise still felt it necessary to give his actors a free hand to "generate and bring to the scene."

Due to either budgetary constraints or the director's preference, a majority of films have no rehearsal time before shooting begins. One of the reasons Altman allowed improvisation was that he insisted on rehearsals, and, therefore, by the time of shooting, the improvisation was well rehearsed. Other directors, such as Frank Capra, wanted no deviation from the script at all. William Friedkin tells of getting into trouble when shooting *The Exorcist* (1973). He scripted ever little movement during rehearsal and insisted on the actors following them exactly. By the time he got to shooting the film, he noticed how flat everything was with no emotion. He immediately told the actors to forget everything he had told them and to just play the character.

Award winning director Andrzej Wajda summarizes the multifaceted collaboration issue this way: "I am fully aware that everything I want to say on the screen has to be filtered through someone else's individuality."[8]

---

8 Elsie M. Walker and David T. Johnson, eds., "Interview with Andrzey Wajda," *Conversations with Directors, An Anthology of Interviews from Literature/Film Quarterly* (Maryland: The Scarecrow Press Inc., 2008), 51.

The following excerpt from a public letter from James Marsh, the director of *The Theory of Everything* (2014), gives a glimpse into the combined art and collaboration:

"The most significant choice I made in the film, like in every other, was in the casting of actors, though the stakes felt much higher this time around. Stephen is an iconic presence in our culture, and most of us have a pretty good idea of what he looks like—and the obvious fact that he doesn't really look like most of us. If the performance struck one bum note anywhere in the film, the film itself wouldn't survive it. So I met Eddie Redmayne, whom I knew had an abundance of talent but had never carried a film of this weight before. During the meeting, he drank a lot more beer than I was expecting—and I saw not only a burning passion to play Stephen but also the right amount of trepidation, which would account for the beer.

It took months and months of preparation, but Eddie became Stephen Hawking across 25 years of inexorable physical decline. On any given day as we filmed, he might be an able-bodied young student, a newly married man struggling with two walking sticks, or a middle-aged man slumped mutely in a wheel chair, barely able to move a finger. The best compliment I can pay him is via Stephen Hawking himself who declared that at some points in the film he thought he was watching himself. He was so taken with Eddie's performance that he offered us the use of his signature electronic voice—so the voice you hear in the movie is his.

This is all well and good but if the other party in this complex love story wasn't able to dance exquisitely in step with Eddie and capture an equal sympathy from an audience very much inclined to sympathize with his character, the film wouldn't work either. Felicity Jones did her own intensive preparation—understanding what it entailed to care for someone in Stephen's condition and the frustrations that come with it. As Eddie mastered the physicality of the role, so did Felicity, uncannily in tune with her partner's body and what it could and couldn't do.

Cinematographer Benoit Delhomme and I wanted to make a visually beautiful film around these performances—using a rich, intense palette of colours and light, taking our cue from Stephen's own good humour and Jane's warmth and optimism in the face of their tribulations. Contriving a gritty and dour realism to convey a disability would have been too obvious and too phony in that context—suiting neither the characters nor the world they lived in.

We have also tried to shine some of our light on to Stephen's scientific ideas—inspired by Isaac Newton and his apple and Archimedes and his bath tub as much as the daunting mathematical language of theoretical physics. The science is at my level of understanding—in the hope that I am as smart (or as dumb) as you are. So I ask forgiveness if I underestimated you—and can only point you in the direction of Errol Morris's excellent film *A Brief History of Time* for further enlightenment. And yet the biggest mystery in our film lies not in the scientific realm but in the inexplicable workings of the human heart. No *Theory of Everything* for that."

Directing: Appreciating the Art

When analyzing the art of a movie's director, consider its composition, lighting, camera placement and movement, and types of shots, then ask yourself the following questions:

- Does the director appear to have a particular style?

- How does he/she reveal that?

- Is there a consistency to the film?

- Is the director's vision communicated to you? Is the message clear?

- Was the director able to get the best performances from the actors?

- Was the interaction between actors well choreographed?

- Considering the fact that the director has the final say over editing, is there a recognizable rhythm or pacing? Are the transitions smooth enough to keep the story's flow?

- Are the various film elements well integrated and cohesive?

CHAPTER TEN

The Cinematographer

The cinematographer transposes the written word into a visual storytelling. Academy Award winner (for *The Godfather* trilogy) Gordon Willis saw himself as a visual psychiatrist using his talent to evoke memories, identification, and emotions: "You are moving the audience around as you see fit" to put them into the right position to see and feel the best performance.

Actor Michael Caine tells the story of watching the day's takes (called the *dailies*) with his director. The director commented that he hadn't seen something Michael did during a scene. When Caine asked him where he was sitting during the take, the director said he was over to the side. To which Caine replied, "That's why you didn't see it. The camera is over here directly in front. You didn't see what the camera saw." In today's digital world, that interchange would not occur because the directors watch the entire shoot on a monitor in order to see *exactly* what the live camera sees. Recall my earlier comment that it is the camera angle, not the viewing angle, that matters.

Another Academy Award cinematographer Vilmos Zsigmond (*Close Encounters of the Third Kind*) suggests that if you consider the director to be the conductor of the orchestra, then the cinematographer is the concertmaster or first violinist. He supervises the camera team, lighting crew, and a team of *grips* who are responsible for moving the cameras and tripods into the right positions. When overhead shots are called for, the grips set up a *dolly* and build tracks, making sure the crane is moved to the correct spot.[1]

In order to attain the meaningful visual design, the cinematographer not only works closely with the director, but also the production designer. The *production designer* guides key personnel in other departments (such as the art department, including construction and decoration; costume designer; key hair and makeup stylists; special effects director; and a locations manager) to establish a unified look for the film. Finally, the cinematographer works with the film editor to make sure the chosen shots contain the right color and correct density for each scene. Cinematographer Vittorio Storaro likes to refer to this group as the "coauthors" along with the screenwriters.

Many times directors insist on working with the same cinematographer on their movies. Among the most notable are Stephen Spielberg with Janusz Kaminski, Ingmar Bergman with Sven Nykvist, Bernardo Bertolucci with Vittorio Storaro, and Orson Welles with Gregg Toland. The same is true for the film editors, although they are less known to the public. Two of the long-time editing combinations are: Martin Scorsese and editor Thelma Schoonmaker (Scorsese at one time was one of Schoonmaker's assistants in the cutting room), and Quentin Tarantino used editor

---

1 A "dolly" is simply a wheeled platform on which the camera is placed. Often the platform runs on a track alongside the character or object being filmed.

Sally Menke on all of his films until she died suddenly in 2010.

Although *The Guardian's* movie critic Jordan Hoffman is only referring to the director, it is obvious the cinematographer had a big part in creating the following described scene in *I Smile Back* (2015): "Laney's rock bottom – well, her first rock bottom anyway – is a nicely photographed haze of pill and booze gobbling mixed with one of the creepiest scenes of self-gratification put to film. Director Adam Salky has an eye for camera placement, holding close on faces and making warm interiors feel menacing."[2] The reviewer believed the movie as a whole was only average, but he made it clear there was an element (the cinematography) that viewers could really appreciate.

Emphasizing that the cinematographer's job is to understand the story and find the images to tell it, three-time Oscar winner Conrad Hall (*Butch Cassidy and the Sundance Kid*, *American Beauty*, *Road to Perdition*) says: "I think visually so that if you turned off the soundtrack, people would stick around and figure out what was going on." Another award winner Haskell Wexler (*Bound for Glory*, *One Flew Over the Cuckoo's Nest*, *Blaze*) described how the lighting used in *Who's Afraid of Virginia Wolf* caused a subliminal effect on the audience.

Three-time Oscar winner Vittorio Storaro (*Apocalypse Now*, *Reds*, *The Last Emperor*) took time off from films to research the meanings of color and light. He published his findings and thoughts in a must-read book for all film

---

2 *The Guardian*, U.S. online version, January 25, 2015.

aficionados: *Writing with Light, Colours, and the Elements*.
According to Storaro, the color scale with meanings is:

"BLACK is the color of Conception

RED is the color of Birth

ORANGE is the color of Growth

YELLOW is the color of Awareness

GRAY is the color of Waiting

GREEN is the color of Knowledge

BLUE is the color of Intelligence

INDIGO is the color of Consciousness

VIOLET is the color of Maturity

the sum of these colors is

WHITE, the color of LIFE."[3]

A simple instance of this in use can be found in *The Last
Emperor* (1987). The movie's first scenes were shot with a red
filter, indicating birth or beginning, then yellow became the

---

3 Vittorio Storaro, Writing with Light, *Colours and the Elements* (Milan, Italy:
Mondadori Electa, 2010).

dominant color as the young emperor becomes aware of his surroundings and position. Peter O'Toole, who played the teacher, brings a bicycle to the palace for the young emperor. Storaro required the bicycle be green. Examples of art within the art.

Other cinematographers use the same colors for other reasons. The most frequent is the use of a yellow tint to convey a time past. (Examples: *The Godfather* and *The Curious Case of Benjamin Button*)

In addition to conveying symbolic meaning as described earlier, color can be used to provide a flow of the narrative and, like hard and soft light, to control the mood and tone of the scene. In *The Curious Case of Benjamin Button* (2008), there is a scene describing how Benjamin's friend Daisy gets hurt. Benjamin is narrating the story and provides a simultaneous description of the facts transitioning back and forth between the story of a woman on the way to work and all the little incidents that occurred in that process and Daisy and her friend at rehearsal. The scenes with Daisy are in full color while the scenes involving the woman have a dark patina that makes the shots appear to be almost in black and white with a touch of color. This tonal distinction aids the viewer in following along by distinguishing the two scenarios.

Lighting

In a May 2004 article in the International Cinematographers Guild (ICG) magazine, writer Bob Fisher reports that just before receiving his first Academy Award for *Apocalypse Now*, Vittorio Storaro said:

> "To me, making a film is like resolving conflicts between light and dark, cold and warmth, blue and orange or other contrasting colors. There should be a sense of energy, or change of movement. A sense that time is going on — light becomes night, which reverts to morning. Life becomes death. Making a film is like documenting a journey and using light in the style that best suits that particular picture... the concept behind it."[4]

The cinematographer's primary tools are the camera with its lenses and set lighting. Although sometimes there may seem to be more, there are only six basic variables to lighting a scene:

- the type of light (i.e., hard or soft);

- the texture;

- the intensity;

- the direction from which it is coming;

---

4 www.cameraguild.com/magazinestool01.htm.

- the height; and

- the color.

For a number of these variables, there are numerous variations on a spectrum. Each lighting variable helps to convey the message of the film. We will not go into the details of the effect of each lighting technique here, but suffice to say that each one can help direct the viewer's attention, show the point of view, and create a mood or emotion. Lighting can also help to soften or exaggerate an actor's natural appearance. Often, just from the contrast and dissolve of the lighting in a particular scene the viewer can begin to figure out what is coming next.

Once the cinematographer has found the desired lighting balance, it is incumbent upon them to maintain a continuity from shot to shot. A change of the camera position must be accomplished without a major change in the light value. Obviously, if sunlight or moonlight is coming through a window, the light will change slightly based upon room location. But if the camera is switching over-the-shoulder shots, there should be no material changes in the lighting. Occasionally a viewer might notice a close-up shot seems brighter. This adds to the viewer's perception of being right in the middle of the conversation. It adds a little more reality of presence.

A hard light properly placed creates shadows. It gives an ominous feel. "The more intense and sharp the Energy vibrant with emotions, such as visible light, the deeper and denser the Shadow. ... Shadow has always been used to visualize the dramas, anxieties and emotions of man."[5] Today's cinematographers learned from old film noir movies how to effectively use single-source lighting and how to use darkness as an important element. For example, diffuse lighting can create a soft, cool feel that subliminally communicates the sense of menace in a character.

The same visual lighting device or effect can have more than one meaning. Dark images may indeed be a sign of danger or evil; they can also reflect a character's emotion, such as sadness or loneliness.

The combination of lighting with creative framing can result in dramatic effects. Consider this excerpt from *New York Times* critic, A. O. Scott's review (May 1, 2014) of *Ida* as he beautifully describes the art found on the screen, reflecting a careful corroboration between cinematographer and director:

> "Filmed in the unusual, boxy aspect ratio of 1.37:1, and most often deployed in static long shots, the film's images sometimes suggest Vermeer lighting with the color taken away, and the compositions manage to seem at once classical and off-handed, with the subjects often located in the screen's two bottom quadrants. As in Bresson, the effect is to draw the viewer's eye into the beauty of the image while simultaneously maintaining a contemplative distance from the drama.

5 Storaro, Writing with Light, Colours and the Elements, 12.

The director never presumes access to the inner lives of his characters. He keeps them low in the frame, with unusually ample space above their heads, creating a kind of cathedral effect. Ida and Wanda can seem small and alone, lost in a vast and empty universe. But their surroundings often achieve a quiet grandeur, an intimation of divine presence."

The following is an excerpt from an interview with Vittorio Storaro that provides tremendous insight into the preproduction process:

"Photography really means writing with light. . . in the sense that I'm trying to express something that is inside of me. With my sensibility, my structure, my cultural background, I'm trying to express what I really am. I am trying to describe the story of the film through the light. I try to have a parallel story to the actual story so that through light and color you can feel and understand, consciously and unconsciously, much more clearly what the story is about.

As soon as I read the script and I speak with the main auteur of the film, the director, and I have the first direction about where the movie should be going, I try to find a way to understand how to conceptualize an image, from the photographic point of view, of the story itself. I try to find what is the main idea and how it can be represented in a symbolic, emotional, psychological, realistic and physical way. That's my approach.

Light is energy. . .Light and color send vibrations back to our body. They affect our metabolism and hence what we perceive. ...Changes of light temperature change the mood and message. ...So you should be very strong in selecting only that kid of light, that kind of tonality, that kind of feeling and that kind of color that you think is right for that story. ...I am talking about the unity of the work itself."[6]

6 Dennis Schaefer and Larry Salvato, *Masters of Light: Conversations with Contemporary Cinematographers* (Oakland: University of California Press, 1984), 219–232.

Cinematography: Appreciating the Art

Ask yourself the following questions when thinking about the cinematography in a film:

- Which scenes stick out in your memory?

- Why those particular scenes?

- What did the cinematographer do to makes these scenes memorable?

- Did you notice special lighting effects? Did these enhance the viewing? Did they help tell the story?

- If there were special color treatments, were they effective?

- Did you notice a difference in lighting between characters? Was this effective?

- Were there some beautifully framed photographic scenes? What was your mental and visceral reaction to them?

CHAPTER ELEVEN

The Film Editor

Many directors consider film editing as "the last phase of screenwriting." This is where the final draft of the script is written. Noted film editor Robert Leighton likened the art of film editing to clay sculpturing. The artist takes a little off, then puts it back in a different shape or size until the flow is just right. While there are, indeed, times editing occurs quickly due to time restraints, the best film editors cut and splice for emotion and meaning. Editing helps create continuity, dramatic focus, tempo, rhythm, mood, narration, and point of view. The average movie has 200 hours of film that has to be cut down to two hours or less. That means that for every minute the audience sees, approximately ninety minutes were tossed. It is not unusual for editing to take up to a year after shooting ends.

But what is editing? It is the art of picking the right frames to join together to make a scene tell a story and then putting those scenes into the right order. Editors use a number of different transition techniques so the story that the director wants to convey appears in the finished product. The number of different editing combinations is dependent upon the number of times the scene was shot, and that can run up to the billions.

The first thing the editor and his team do is to remove all of the footage containing errors. Then assembly begins by picking the best frame for each shot and starting to group them. Once the frames are chosen, they are then put together in what is, hopefully, a coherent way to create the meaningful narrative. Sometimes a scene is intended for a particular place in a movie, but after viewing the clean shots the editor decides that moving it somewhere else will add something extra to the film. The next stage involves cutting hours and minutes out of the film and deciding upon the proper transitions. Are you beginning to see the art involved in editing?

Post-production editing involves images, sound and music. The process is used for the director and the various editors to get the one that is just right. Sometimes, however, that means assembling from a number of shots or sounds. The order selection in and of itself conveys a message and tells a story in a particular way.

Perhaps the part of the process the average viewer will notice most is the transitions. The most common is a *cut*. Cuts do not change scenes, just the viewing angles. For example, as an audience member, you are looking over the shoulder of one character talking to another. Then there is a cut so that now you are looking over the shoulder of the second character back at the first character. The cuts need to be meaningful and convey an emotion or idea.

If there is a change of time or place, a *dissolve* transition is often used, such as when one shot is superimposed over another and as it begins to dissolve, the next shot starts to appear through the fade. Or as the dissolve is completing, the new shot appears with no break. The third most common type of transition is a *fade*, in which one scene fades to black, and then a new time and place appear with perhaps different characters.

If the transitions are not done properly, the pace is broken, the mood is destroyed, and the viewer can become disoriented. Chop up the story in the wrong place, and the movie's "spell" is broken. Even the most inexperienced moviegoer notices poor editing.

The famous scene of Meg Ryan faking an orgasm in *When Harry Met Sally* (1989) did not occur exactly as it appears in the film. That scene was shot over sixty times. Director Rob Reiner and film editor Robert Leighton took tiny snippets and put them together to create the most compelling final scene by taking a particular "ooh" from one shot, a sniff from another, a deep breath from yet another take, etc., etc. Ironically, the most famous line from the movie and one listed in the top 100 famous lines by the American Film Institute (AFI) is: "I'll have whatever she's having," which was spoken by Reiner's mother, singer Estelle Lebost.

One of my favorite dissolve-editing accomplishments can be found in Spike Lee's *Mo' Better Blues* (1990). One can barely detect the dissolve because it is done so skillfully. Bleek, played by Denzel Washington, has been two-timing two women, and each believes she is his only girlfriend. After they both show up at the club at the same time, in the same dress, Bleek has a dream about making love with each of them. The dream merges events into a single bedroom scene. Close-ups of each woman fade into the other woman as she comes across his body. The lines are broken up with each actress speaking part of the line.

In fact, Washington was not in any of the takes with either woman; he was edited in. The two women spoke his lines for each other to get through the shot. The editor then edited the video and the sound into a collage; the effect was so perfectly timed, it was hard for the viewer to immediately realize that the picture and sound had changed. The impact of each woman venting her anger and love at Bleek was tremendous. It was never a gimmicky scene, but a meaningful emotional scene. A masterful editing job.

In *Vertigo* (1958), Jimmy Stewart is helping the woman he loves put on a necklace. The camera zooms into a shot in the mirror showing the necklace around her neck, and then the camera slowly pulls back to show that necklace is now on another woman in a painting. This is called a *match cut*, and it creates a shock effect and suspense. Alfred Hitchcock always preferred suspense over surprise. Suspense involved the viewer in the action and kept them waiting for the answer.

Film editor Walter Murch has won two Academy Awards (*The English Patient* and *Apocalypse Now*) and been nominated for five others. He describes an ideal cut as "one that satisfies all of the following six criteria at once:

1.   It is true to the emotion of the moment;

2.   It advances the story;

3.   It occurs at a moment that is rhythmically interesting and 'right';

4. It acknowledges what you might call 'eye-trace' – the concern with the location and movement of the audience's focus of interest within the frame;

5. It requires 'planarity,' the grammar of three dimensions transposed by photography to two;

6. ...[I]t respects the three-dimensional continuity of the actual space (where people are in the room and in relation to one another)."[1]

When deciding which are most important to not lose, Murch ranks the six as follows:

1.	Emotion	51%
2.	Story	23%
3.	Rhythm	10%
4.	Eye-trace	7%
5.	Two-dimensional plane of screen	5%
6.	Three-dimensional space of action	4%

If the editor finds that he/she has to sacrifice certain of the six things to make a cut, "sacrifice your way up, item by

1 Walter Murch, *In the Blink of an Eye: A Perspective of Film Editing*, 2nd ed. (Los Angeles: Silman James Press, 2001), 18.

item, from the bottom."[2] As discussed throughout this book, emotion always trumps other considerations.

Film Editing: Appreciating the Art
Ask yourself the following questions about a film's editing:

- Does the editing help me follow the story and journey through the movie experience?

- Does it jump too much, leaving me in the lurch and wondering where I am or what is happening?

- Is the mode used visually comfortable or irritating?

- Is the music editing appropriate? Does it stop and start at the right times? Is it part of the storytelling or just background music?

- And, as Murch emphasizes, are the emotion and story left intact?

---

2 Ibid., 19.

CHAPTER TWELVE

Film Techniques

Each of the artists responsible for the various elements in a film uses a number of techniques to convey their own vision as tempered by the director's vision. Each technique, element, and process can be used for different purposes, depending upon the situation presented. One example I recall from my film classes is the use of columns. Shot from below on the front of a city hall or similar building, columns connote strength and power of the government. If the columns are at the top of many stairs, they imply a courthouse and the legal system. Yet columns used on front of a large house suggest a fancy residence owned by wealthy people.

As I have pointed out earlier, it is ultimately the director's vision of how each technique, element, and process should be used to control the outcome. There are exceptions to this rule, such as when the director has ultimate trust in the ability and experience of the supporting technical artist. Also, a number of directors allow the actors to develop characters with their own interpretation. The negative exception to the rule is when a director is not established enough to demand the final cut of his or her film in the contract, and the studio and/or producers change the tenor of the movie to what *they* think will sell. In almost every case in which that happens, it is the viewers and the art that suffer.

Point of View

One aspect that determines which technique to use is the *point of view*. From whose point of view is the story being told? There are three primary character points of view that can be utilized in film:

1. A narrator's, who may or may not be seen on the screen, point of view is used by providing a voice-over or beginning to tell a story on screen and then having the story proceed on screen with the viewer in role of a somewhat-removed observer.

2. A first-person point of view is presented through a character who best serves the writer's purpose.

3. The third point of view is an objective one, letting the viewer be part of the scene but with no emphasis on any character's perspective.

The point of view may also change within a scene or as the film progresses. It may even change several times, going back and forth. This allows the viewers to identity with a number of characters in the film and makes us feel things are more real. It helps transpose us into the action itself. Another point of view taking place in a film is the narrative perspective, which is the point of view from which a story is being told. As part of the structure of the story, perspective helps to shape meaning. It becomes a value system the audience is asked to accept.

In his book *On Film-making: An Introduction to the Craft of the Director*, Alexander Mackendrick asks:

"Who is your point of view character? Sometimes it can be difficult to decide between who is the protagonist and who is the antagonist. Though occasionally there are stories in which the audience is not invited to feel identification with any of the characters, it is far more common to have a figure who represents the viewpoint of the story and who has a final 'objective' of some kind. Ask yourself: by the end of the story what does this character want to achieve? What is required is a character intention that will produce a dramatic action, a visible result onscreen....[F]or a character merely to express his or her feelings is seldom enough in cinema. There can be, of course, a negative objective to prevent something from happening, but this too should be conceived as a result of action...."[1]

Mise-en-scène and Framing

The arrangement of everything that appears in the framing—the actors, lighting, space, decor, props, costumes—is called *mise-en-scène*, a French term that means "staging or putting on an action or scene." (It is also called a full-screen shot.) The frame, its composition, and the camera work also constitute part of the *mise-en-scène* of a movie. The *mise-en-scène* is the end result of the efforts

---

1 Alexander Mackendrick, *On Film-making: An Introduction to the Craft of the Director* (New York: Faber and Faber, 2004), 20.

of many professionals. It is what appears within a shot or a scene and where the audience's experience begins.

The *mise-en-scène* encompasses the relationship between the film elements and affects the viewer's perception, mood, and emotions. When looking at a scene, consider whether or not the combination of all these elements aid your understanding of the story and/or the characters. Does the *mise-en-scène* convey meaning of the shot or scene? Occasionally, the *mise-en-scène* will create the impression of something opposite to what you expected. This might be intentional, such as in a suspense movie that is giving you false clues. The majority of the time, however, it is complementary to the narrative. Pay attention to everything you see in a shot because something on the fringe of that shot might be a clue to what will come or may help explain something.

Another technique to be aware of is the frame composition. When composing a shot, what the director or cinematographer choose to frame has a direct impact on the viewer's emotional response. The placement of the frame has a certain effect on the characters and a different effect on the viewers. A tight, close-in frame places constraints on the characters movements—they are trapped, literally and figuratively. The viewers, however, are pulled into the shot and experience an intimacy with the scene. They become a part of the event, not just spectators. Using a *closed-frame composition* pulls our focus into the frame and leads to a stronger emotional response because there is no thought of what might be outside the frame. *Son of Saul* (2015) was shot on 35mm. film using a 45mm. lens. Cinematographer

Mátyás Erdély then used a very soft focus blurring most of what was behind the character(s). The overall effect was that the viewer feels squeezed into the location with no room to explore. It is very dramatic and effective at conveying the message.

In contrast, an *open-frame composition* lets the viewer wander around the entire frame and implies there is more than we can see. A wide, open shot allows for the development of the scene. It denotes a certain freedom for the actors and the cameraman. The viewer is now more of an observer waiting to be directed. There is an underlying tension waiting to be released. The classic scene of all the wounded soldiers lying side by side in the train yard in *Gone With the Wind* (1939) makes us believe that more people are there, but we just cannot see them. Compare that scene with the scene in *Ida* (2014), in which we are drawn straight into the frame and made to feel restricted as to where we can look. Everything you need is within the frame.

In either type of shot, the amount of space a character receives could be reflective of his/her importance or dominance over the others. Negative space, which is just as important, might also denote loneliness, anguish, or depression. By using the camera's point of view, the viewer's attention could be directed to an object or figure in the background. Regardless of where the camera points your attention, one should always take note of the background. There are often significant clues that can be useful in understanding the movie.

Gone With The Wind – MGM/Photofest

Ida – Opus Film/Photofest - 2013

In *Vagabond* (1985), director Agnès Varda used an unusual technique to carry the viewer along the movie's journey: a combination of music and repetitive images are meant to connect viewers to the scenes. The music was divided into twelve parts and was only heard as the lead character, played by Sandrine Bonnaire, walked from one location to another. The shots were all shot using dollies.

Each dolly scene ends with a shot of an object, such as a farm instrument or a tire. The next dolly shot, which occurs several minutes later, starts out with an image of the same type of object as Bonnaire continues her journey. In the supplemental feature on the DVD, Varda explained her reasoning exactly as Münsterberg would have expected: "I thought the eye might memorize things. A sort of persistence of vision whereby people would have sensed or guessed that the dolly shots were connected." While this technique was an interesting artistic expression by Varda and assisted in scene continuity, it was not essential to the viewer's understanding of the movie.

Camera Lenses, Focal Length, and Angles

The type of lens a cinematographer has a cameraman use will affect the look of the image. There are three primary types of shots in a movie: a long shot, a medium shot, and a close-up—with variations on either side of each of them. How these shots ultimately look varies, depending on the type of lenses used and the angle of the camera.

Long shots are often used as an establishing shot. They show an entire setting and the relationship of a person or object to that setting. After that, the camera then moves in closer for a medium or close-up shot. The medium shot, while narrowing down the viewer's focus, still shows some relationship of the characters to the environment. The close-up shot primarily focuses on characters or objects, and allows the viewer to enter the scene and experience a visceral or emotional response. In other words, as the camera distance changes, the director is manipulating the viewers by directing their attention, providing perception, and affecting their emotions. As the camera gets into the viewer's personal space, the viewer gets into the character's space. As the camera placement moves, the viewer gets to focus on things like facial expressions, eye contact, and body position, all of which help illustrate the interaction between the character and others in the scene. These gestures are just another element of the storytelling. The expressiveness of the human face can often tell so much more than dialogue.

The *focal length* of a lens determines how much magnification it provides. For example, a long focal length can make an object appear to be much closer than it really is. The shorter the focal length, the wider the shot. The longer the focal length, the more the shot is zoomed in. Put another way, a shorter focal length has greater optical power. A 50mm focal length is the equivalent of what the average eye sees. Most viewers will not be able to determine which focal length was used in a particular shot.

In *Short Term 12* (2013) there are many close-up and medium-close shots. I met two of the actors at a film festival and asked if that inhibited their acting. They told me that, for some of the shots, the camera was almost on their cheeks and they just had to block it out and go on with the scene. However, when the action in the scene was of an intimate nature, the shot was taken with a long lens, such as a 300mm, that gave the same impact on the screen. But most importantly, since the camera was farther away, the actors had more room to move and act.

Many directors prefer to shoot in a wide-screen (anamorphic) mode, which affects how a shot will look.[2] Sidney Pollack (*Tootsie, Out of Africa, The Firm*) said that the reason he used wide screen was to "compose frames that have enormous tension and movement in them, to shoot pictures that need a sense of place."[3] Compare this with Martin Scorsese (*Mean Streets, Goodfellas, Wolf of Wall Street*), who feels that "wide angle' lenses give more depth of field, more perspective, more richness to the shot, which is opposite of a 'flat' look."[4]

Most directors do not like using zoom lenses. They feel a zoom lens lacks the sharpness of a prime lens, and the result is film that looks much flatter. Scorsese tells of occasionally zooming in to create the appearance of the camera moving when there wasn't physical room to actually move it. Wide shots give the actors a little more freedom in their movements. Even medium shots can give actors more freedom. "There's a certain freedom in *Goodfellas* (1990), as it's mostly medium shots, where the actors have room to move. But that's the world these characters live in. It's not

---

2 Wide screen and wide angle are not the same. Anamorphic increases the sides of the frame but not the vertical aspect. Wide angle increases both the sides and the height. It is a long-distance shot.

3 Tirard, Moviemakers' *Master Class*, 170.

4 Ibid., 65.

a world of close-ups. They have people around them all the time, and what they do always affects the world around them. So you have to shoot it in medium shots." [5]

It was also in *Goodfellas*, however, that Scorsese used a technique that is discussed in almost every beginning film class: Henry and Jimmy are seated in a booth at a diner. There is a window behind them and one can see the restaurant and parking lot across the street. The shot has deep focus.[6] The camera tracks backward while also zooming in. The two men stay within the frame in the same position, but become larger as the background also gets larger, more compressed, and slightly out of focus. Now the two men are the sole focus of the shot. The shot goes from a normal scene to something more intense. There is emotion conveyed and the beginning of some meaning to the scene. The viewer goes from being an observer to feeling as if he/she is a participant.

The second phase of the camera position is the angle. Once again, we find three primary positions: low, high, and medium, which is usually eye level. A low shot, meaning the camera angle is looking up, usually creates a perception of strength or power in the character or object. It can also help create fear. A high shot is similar to a long shot from above, providing a view of the character in relation to the scene. In some cases, it is used to show desolation or the beauty or barrenness of the countryside. In other shots, it can

---

5 Ibid., 67.

6 "Deep focus" is the focusing of a filmed scene to make both close and distant objects equally clear.

convey vulnerability, weakness, isolation, or helplessness of the character.

In the opening shots of both Orson Welles' *Touch of Evil* (1958) and Robert Altman's *The Player* (1992), a single take uses all three types of shots and all three angles. There is another angle that is occasionally used called "canted," in which the camera is tilted to one side or another. This shot is derived from early movies whose photography was based upon German expressionism.

In celluloid film days, the longest a film shot could be was ten minutes, because that was all the film in the cartridge. In his 1948 film, *Rope*, Alfred Hitchcock amazed the industry when he decided to shoot the film in what would appear to be one long, continuous "take" without cutaways or any other breaks in the action. Since it was celluloid, the film did, in fact, have cleverly disguised breaks every ten minutes. Today, by shooting digitally, the entire movie can be a single shot. *Birdman* (2014) has the appearance of being a single shot with no cuts or fades for the entire movie. Again the critics are raving—probably because most are too young to know about Hitchcock's *Rope*. If you start to wonder about "how they got that shot," there is a good chance it was not real but done digitally with computer assistance.

Filmmakers guide the viewer's attention, perception, and emotion through camera placement, lens length, focus and depth of field, and lighting. The following description of the camera work and framing in *The Guardian*, critic Peter Bradshaw's review of *A Pigeon Sat on a Branch Reflecting on Existence* (2015) is an excellent example of what can be accomplished to create a tone and mood:

> "Figures and faces are seen in the middle-distance, never close-up, but with pin-sharp clarity; [Director] Andersson maintains a rigorous deep focus all along his vertiginous perspective lines, so that we can see the figures on the distant skyline, or buildings from a rear window, in the same painterly detail as a scuffed table in the foreground. Each interrelated scene is a vivid, eerily complete world: perhaps like the "magic lantern" displays in the Thorne Miniature Rooms at the Chicago Art Institute, which famously inspired Orson Welles."

The number and different types of techniques used by all of the contributors to a film is obviously too much to cover in a beginner's movie-appreciation guide. As you watch more films, you will begin to notice and appreciate the various techniques. I encourage you to consult a film school textbook for more technical explanations.

Compare the two shots from *Clouds of Sils Maria*. Same location, different angle and depth. The top shot is an establishing shot. It shows the grandeur of the location and the smallness of the characters against the grandeur. The bottom shot is at the same location but the camera has moved to front side. The viewer still sees the mountain in the background to reaffirm where the characters are but now the mid close-up changes the viewers' focus to the emotion in the people's faces. A different story being told.

Publicity stills: *Clouds of Sils Maria*,
CG Cinema et al / Sundance Selects (2014)

Phoenix (2014) Schramm Film Koerner & Weber / Sundance Selects

As the camera is even closer in this shot from *Phoenix*, the viewer is made to feel as if they are standing right in the shot. The looks on each actor's face conveys the emotion and story. Each one is looking for something different.

Publicity still: *Short Term 12* (2013) Animal Kingdom / Demarest Films

In the lower picture again the viewer is pulled into the scene. Note how Brie Larson is crisp and clear while Keith Stanfield is blurred. This draws attention directly to Larson narrowing the viewer's focus even more.

PART FOUR

Analyzing Films

CHAPTER THIRTEEN

Where You View the Film Counts

Does it matter where you view the film and the size of the screen? The simple answer to both questions is, "Yes."

The best place to watch digital films is in a theater with wide screens, high resolution projectors and high definition sound. The majority of today's films are shot and processed for these environments. Some directors, however, are still using film stock for a richer, soft feel with some grain. Recent examples are *Ida* (2013) which was shot on 35mm film in a 1.33 to 1 ratio, *Carol* (2015) shot on 16mm film and *Son of Saul* (2015) shot on 35mm film in 1:37 to 1 ratio which all need to be watched using a 35mm projector to get the full impact. Unfortunately few theaters still have these projectors. Thankfully a few did save them when making the conversion to digital. When The Hateful Eight (2015) was released in its 70mm film format, many theaters had to rent correct projectors and wider screens to show it.

IMAX, while providing a larger image closer to the audience, is only meant for particular types of movies. The most common are those with a great deal of computerized special effects and graphics. Some of the more standard movies are attempting to use the IMAX format in order to gain better depth, such as in 3D.

Contrary to the marketing images of Apple, Samsung, Dell, et al, with the exception of some *avant-garde* shorts, films are not made to be viewed on small screens. The full picture providing the full impact cannot be seen on a phone, tablet, or computer monitor. The nuances are always lost. Often part of the shot is eliminated. Filmmaker Spike Lee, speaking at Ebertfest 2014, was adamant that films are meant to be seen projected on a screen: "That's criminal! Criminal, to watch a movie on an iPhone...We work too hard for the sound and the cinematography means everything to the movie."

Director James Cameron (*Titanic, Avatar*), who specializes in making epic features, agrees: "If someone wants to watch it on a [phone], I'm not going to stop them, especially if they are paying for it. I think it's dumb, when you have characters that are so small in the frame that they're not visible...To me, there's a limit that you wouldn't want to go below...I've never watched *Avatar* on a laptop...I don't recommend it." [1]

The only native widescreen ratio supported by DVD is 16:9. DVD makers can show the higher ratios in a 16:9 frame by adding black bars around the image. When using digital formats, a scope extraction is used to show the film on TV or DVD, resulting in a shorter height being viewed, which changes the entire perspective of the shot. A scene shot using a wide-angle format will end up looking like a close-up in the squeezed version.

With the move into 2K and 4K video-capture standards, the difficulty of watching on a small screen is increased. (2K and 4K are resolution levels. a K represents 1024 pixels,

---

[1] James Cameron, *James Cameron: Interviews (Conversations with Filmmakers Series)*, Brent Dunham, ed. (Jackson: University Press of Mississippi, 2012), 204.

so a 2K image is 2048 pixels horizontally. The higher the resolution, the smaller things are on the screen and the more there is in the frame. Some stores market the higher resolutions as "Super High Def." The average 17" computer monitor is 1280 pixels or just slightly more than 1K. When your TV manual talks about images being 720 or 1080, it refers to the number of video lines measured vertically. The more lines, the sharper the picture, but again the smaller the objects or people.)

Watching a film on a small television (45" or less) is a definite improvement over a computer or tablet, but it is, unfortunately, still lacking. The nuances in color, shadowing, and framing do not show up clearly due to the cramped image. If you put the higher resolution on these televisions, it makes the objects appear to be smaller. This seems unfair, particularly for apartment dwellers who have smaller rooms, but I do not foresee any attempt to technologically compensate forthcoming.

The larger screens (50" to 72") combined with a 5:1 surround sound or larger provide the best home option for most viewers. The filmmakers' intended effects can usually be seen at this ratio. While editing, many directors and editors today view the film on a fifty-inch screen. Also, by having the larger screen area, these televisions can utilize higher resolutions that provide truer colors and greater clarity. This enhances the emotional communication with the viewer.

The ultimate home-viewing option is a big-screen television (82" to 110") with a 7:1 surround sound home-theater arrangement. This arrangement puts you as close as possible to the in-theater experience. The full picture in very high resolution is usually possible with this setup. The sound encompasses the room and will grip you. Sadly, this is also the most expensive solution and requires a large room. Hence, few can entertain the thought of having this arrangement.

CHAPTER FOURTEEN

Looking for Meaning

Now that you have some idea of how the meaning is conveyed, the next task is to develop a system for determining the actual meaning(s) found within any given film. All films display some obvious meaning on the surface. But most are not that simple, and directors go out of their way to put deeper meanings into their films. As previously discussed, in order to transport you into the world of the story, the filmmakers use narrative and visuals that are influenced by lighting, color, movement, camera angles, performance, and then the editing. Add the effect of sets, costumes, and makeup, and you forget that you are being manipulated into an artificial form of reality.

> A film's meaning is conveyed to the viewer through the interplay of all of the film's elements. The way each and every element is used in each frame occurs for a specific reason. The viewer is left to determine what narrative is being conveyed through the interplay.

Utilizing Münsterberg's six key processes (perception, attention, memory, imagination, suggestion, and emotions) and noting how various elements are used to direct your attention or convey a message, you will be able to discern the meanings by analyzing the films you watch.

Filmmakers use many techniques to convey meaning that the average person does not usually recognize immediately. It is a subliminal process. You now know what to look for in terms of the techniques, so now let us look at ways of discerning both the explicit and the implicit meanings. Film theorist Deborah Thomas posits that a "film's meanings are thus not so much a set of propositions which can be readily detached from the film but rather a complex combination of themes and their simultaneous embodiments in a number of elements."[1]These elements include first and foremost the *mise-en-scène*, the sound and look, performance and narrative, camera use, and the film's overall structure and tone as provided by the editing. The analysis of *Lone Star* in the next chapter demonstrates all of these elements.

In order to identify and appreciate the unique art presented in a film one must become actively involved with the characters and story. Your mind, eyes, ears, and emotions must engage in an interplay with the images and sounds before you. Your life experiences, along with the expectations you hold of a particular actor or director or genre, often affect your perception and judgment of a film. It will become necessary to overcome these presets to open yourself up to accepting what is presented free of such restraints and just experience the film.

---

1 Deborah Thomas, *Reading Hollywood: Spaces and Meanings in American Film* (London, England: Wallflower Press, 2001).

While watching a film for the first time, you cannot point out particular shots or lines of dialogue and fully appreciate their ultimate relationship to the entirety of the picture. Only when the film has ended, and sometimes not even that soon, can your memory and the other processes begin to work to see the whole. Once you have sorted out the full message intended by the filmmaking team, the time to filter it through your own value systems begins. Away from the stimulus of the film, you are better able to tie words, events, and all that was present in a given *mise-en-scéne* together and begin to assimilate and interpret. Certainly, not all films provide for deeper reflection and discovery. Some are formulaic, cookie cutter, fluff. Others provide real insight into human nature and realistic problems. The majority lie somewhere within that continuum.

Movies contain a number of layers of meaning, and it becomes easier to find and interpret them once you become a proactive viewer. Sometimes we can ascertain the cultural values, biases, and opinions of the director that are below the surface. The most difficult are those meanings the director infers from an implied situation. The resulting inference will be affected by our own experiences. This is inevitable and the reason why there is so often disagreement over what a movie is about. If a movie touches an emotional spot in you, you will likely appreciate the film and feel warmed or excited by it. The viewer who was not emotionally touched will be less enthusiastic.

When a viewer walks out of a movie, the first thing they ask themselves is, "Did I like it?" The answer could be a simple "Yes" or "No," or it could be more complex, such as:

"I sort of liked it. I liked the emphasis on the relationship between the two, but didn't like how long it took to find out what was going on." Perhaps, the response might be, "I didn't really care for the movie, but I was deeply moved by the music and the acting."

What are these reactions based on? Was the viewer not adequately entertained? Did they not understand the message, or was the message not to their liking? Were they confused or bored? Did the filmmakers fail in their mission? There obviously could be a multitude of reasons for any reaction.

As you watch a scene and see something you don't understand or that seems unusual, make a note to think about it after the movie. Later, when you start to consider what you have seen, ask yourself if you learned the answer by the end of the film. As part of your exploration, ask yourself: "Why was that in the scene, or why was the scene in the movie?"

"Meaning in movies is also created through metaphor, structure, character and motifs. In a metaphor, a thing is associated with a similar idea or an emotional state. Structure describes the overall design of a movie, the way different elements balance one another. Characters are created by screenwriters and given life by actors. Their development–from ignorance to enlightenment or fear to courage–is often a way making meaning in movies. Finally, meaning is created through motifs or repetitive elements such as objects that evoke themes, feelings or ideas." [2]

---

2 Michael Ryan and Melissa Lenos,, *An Introduction to Film Analysis: Technique and Meaning in Narrative Film* (London, England: Bloomsbury Academic Publishing, 2012), 133.

A *metaphoric image* is a single image containing two representative elements used to link the different ideas together. It becomes stronger than one depicting either part of the metaphor on its own. As pointed out earlier, a film is the sum of its elements, and those elements complement each other either positively or negatively. This provides the structure of the film. Every character should be there for a reason. Finding that reason will help you to find meaning. A motif as used in the above quote means a theme that runs through all or part of a film.

What is the subject matter of the film's messages? Some messages may come from a humanistic event, possibly including psychological, social, political, cultural, philosophical, or moral issues. Be sure to use the genre to aid in your determination. Gender, racial, and ethnic statements are frequent subjects for films. In any given film, more than one of these approaches may be used. It might have been only in one scene or several scenes rather than throughout the entire movie. The viewer may not appreciate or agree with the position taken in the story, but if that position is presented fairly, consistently, and clearly, then perhaps the director's goals have been met.

Which elements or scenes provided a strong emotional or sensual reaction? Specifically, what was the emotion, and what was in the frame that caused it? In other words, how did I respond to the *mise-en-scène*? Why did I react that way? If your answer points to any of the elements discussed in this book, that indicates you are appreciating the film's art even if you don't realize it. A broader consideration is to determine how each of the elements, individually and combined, helped to convey the theme and tone and bring about a reaction. Which elements were stronger, and did they contribute more to your appreciation of the film? Were some weak and detract from your enjoyment?

Other ways of reaching an appreciation of the art is to determine whether or not you gained a better understanding of the subject or an insight into interpersonal relationships— or perhaps, a greater insight to the workings of the mind. If you did, then the film was successful at some level.

As the previous chapters have noted, meanings are found in mood and tone, what a character is thinking, visual images, music, location, and time. All of these elements help you find answers to the above questions. Sometimes, what *wasn't* said or shown actually contains the answer. Deep, serious thought is required. Appreciation of the art you have experienced will not happen in the immediate response at the conclusion of the film. It takes time to sift through the many frames that flew by you at the rate of twenty-four per second. An introspective analysis followed by a second viewing will provide the greatest identification and appreciation. However, since most people do not have time or means for a second viewing, then honing the requisite skills through the viewing of many films will have to provide the solution.

The Meaning: Appreciating the Art

Questions to ask yourself as you seek meaning in any film you watch:

- Were there any recurring narrative or visual patterns? If so what did they convey? Why were they recurring?

- Can I identify the explicit theme(s)?

- Did I recognize the implicit themes(s)?

- What were the various themes?

- What element(s) led me to recognize them?

- Was I convinced?

- Was the film successful in conveying a point of view through the characters, the actions, or the tone?

CHAPTER FIFTEEN

Film Analyses

To help illustrate how I analyze a film, the next section contains discussions of four films: *Lone Star* (1996), *Tell No One* (2006), *Amour* (2012), and *The Book Thief* (2013). *Tell No One* and *The Book Thief* are both adaptations of novels. The other two are original screenplays written by the film's director. All of them involve quality filmmaking with each garnering several awards and other nominations. If you have not previously done so, I recommend that you watch each of these films for a feast of cinematic art and to better understand the analyses.

The section examines certain parts of the movies to show how information from the previous sections of this book will help you gain a better understanding of a film's meanings and the actual art displayed by the various filmmakers. It is important to remember that you are not being given a complete synopsis or analysis. The focus is only on portions of the films.

The first analysis, *Lone Star*, is more in-depth than the others for the reasons:

1. *Lone Star* has more themes to find and discuss than most films;

2.   I wanted this analysis to cover as much of the
     material covered in this book as possible.

3.   I had a copy of the shooting script that enabled me
     to see the notes and instructions writer/director
     John Sayles had placed in it.

This level of probing, hopefully, prepares you for working
with those films that are less complex in their presentation.
Each movie lends itself to a slightly different analysis
approach and I have tried to show that in the analyses
that follow.

LONE STAR (1996)
- Written, directed, and edited by John Sayles
- Distributed by: Columbia Pictures and Castle Rock

PRIMARY CHARACTERS:

- **Sam Deeds**: Current sheriff
- **Buddy Deeds**: Sam's father and a former sheriff. He was previously a deputy under Charley Wade.
- **Charley Wade**: Former sheriff and boss of Buddy and Hollis
- **Hollis**: Current mayor and former deputy for both Buddy and Charley
- **Mercedes Cruz**: Owner of the Mexican restaurant and Pilar's mother
- **Pilar**: Sam's high school love and daughter of Mercedes Cruz the owner of the Mexican restaurant
- **Big O (Otis)**: Owner of the black bar and Del's father
- **Del**: Big O's son and the new colonel assigned to the local base.

FROM THE CRITICS:

Roger Ebert in the *Chicago Sun Times*, July 3, 1996:

"*Lone Star* contains so many riches, it humbles ordinary movies. ... It is only later, thinking about the film, that we appreciate the full reach of the material."

Janet Maslin in the New York Times, June 21, 1996:

"Gratifyingly complex and beautifully told, this tale explores a huge array of cultural, racial, economic and family tensions. In the process, it also sustains strong characters, deep emotions and clear dramatic force."

SYNOPSIS

Reminiscent of a fine novel in depth and complexity, writer-director John Sayles' acclaimed drama uses the investigation of a twenty-five-year-old murder as the framework for a detailed exploration of life in a Texas border town. The nominal center of the film is Sheriff Sam Deeds, the chief law officer of the town of Frontera. The low-key Sam is also the son of the late Buddy Deeds, who also served as town sheriff and still maintains a legendary status for ousting the vicious, corrupt Charley Wade. The discovery of Wade's decades-old skeleton, however, calls this legend into question, and forces Sam to begin an investigation.

During this search for the truth, Sam must come to terms with his own troubled emotions about his father and his still-lingering romantic feelings for Pilar, a Hispanic woman Buddy had prevented him from seeing as a young man. *Lone Star*'s scope encompasses not only this story but the whole town, addressing Pilar's difficulties as a schoolteacher, the conflict between incoming immigrants and border patrol officers, and the troubles faced by the African-American commander of the local military base.

Sayles expertly moves between past and present, weaving his stories together to illustrate how the seemingly disparate parts of a community are in fact intimately interconnected. Raising issues of race, politics, and identity, *Lone Star* nevertheless focuses most of its attention on its complex, believable characters that are performed well by an excellent ensemble cast.

ANALYSIS

Determining a single genre for this film is difficult because it encompasses so much. It is a mystery, a drama, a romance, and a border film. It deals with history, personal identity, cultural relationships, politics, corruption, and individual morality. The key stories are a murder investigation, a love that has never been extinguished, and three parent-child relationships. The themes found in the film are murder/mystery, politics/corruption, love, multiculturalism, racism, illegal entry into United States, troubled parent-child relationships, the effects of divorce, and incest.

Through the excellent camera work, dialogue, and directing, we the viewers come to know and identify with the former and present residents of Frontera, a fictitious town located in Rio County in South Texas.

The movie opens with the soft Mexican music of a guitar. After the opening scene a more robust Mexican song plays over the titles. Through the music and the opening scene the setting has been established as the U.S. side of the Mexican border.

In the opening scene human remains are found on an old army shooting range. A clue to the identity of the remains is a Masonic ring found by the bones. A little later, a badge that turns out to be that of a Rio County sheriff is found nearby. We meet the current Sheriff Sam Deeds as he pulls up to investigate.

The scene now switches to a school where a Mexican teacher (Pilar) is assuring a black mother that her son is not in trouble. As they talk, Pilar receives a message that her own son cut school that day. Through the dialogue in this scene, we learn that the class is predominately Mexican with some whites and a few blacks. The cultural mix of the community has been established for the viewer.

The film then quickly moves to a Mexican restaurant where Frontera's Mayor Hollis is holding forth with two friends, eating lunch and telling a story about Buddy Deeds. Following the classic American scriptwriter's rule, this six-minute scene begins six minutes into the movie and provides links to several of the film's themes. The initial shot is a medium-close shot of all three men, but, thereafter, the shots are individual close-ups. What follows are excerpts from the script.

FENTON: Won't be another like him. That boy of his doesn't come near it. You ask me, he's all hat and no cattle.

SAM (Off Screen.): Fellas–

(WIDEN to see Sam standing by their booth. No telling how long he's been listening, Fenton is embarrassed.)

HOLLIS: Sam! I was just telling a few about your old man.

FENTON: He was a unique individual.

SAM: Yeah, he was that.

(We sense a little strain when Sam has to talk about his father–)

HOLLIS: Big day coming up--I wish we'd have thought of it while he was still living. But he went so unexpected.

FENTON: Better late than never. Korean War hero, Sheriff for near thirty years–Buddy Deeds Memorial P--

SAM: I heard there was a bit of a fuss.

HOLLIS: Oh, you know, the usual troublemakers. Danny Padilla from the Sentinel, that crowd.

FENTON: Every other damn thing in the country is called after Martin Luther King, they can't let our side have one measly courthouse?

HOLLIS: King wasn't Mexican, Fenton–

FENTON: Bad enough all the street names are in Spanish–

SAM: They were here first.

FENTON: Then name it after Big Chief Shitinabucket! Whoever that Tonkawa fella was. He had the Mexes beat by centuries.

Hollis is then asked to tell the story of Charley Wade's disappearance and how Buddy Deeds became sheriff. As Hollis begins to tell his story, the camera aims down at his hands, which are next to a basket of tortillas. The light dims slightly and a different song starts playing, which is a signal to some sort of change in the scene. As the camera continues to pan, a hand reaches into the basket from the other side, lifts a tortilla, and removes some money. The hand has a Masonic ring on it. Further panning and a tilt up reveals the hand belongs to Charley Wade, who boasts about getting his cut to leave the restaurant owner's illegal workers, whom he calls "wetbacks," alone. Wade sits across from his two deputies Hollis and Buddy. He tells Buddy that it will be his job to pick up the money in the future.

BUDDY: I'm not picking it up.

WADE: You do whatever I say you do or else you put it on the trail, son.

Columbia Pictures/Castle Rock:
Camera is low looking up at Wade giving him appearance of power.

(The CUSTOMERS are all watching now, nervous. Buddy thinks for a moment, not taking his eyes off Wade.)

BUDDY: How 'bout this--how 'bout you put that shield on this table and vanish before you end up dead or in jail?

Columbia Pictures/Castle Rock

(Wade rests his hand on his pistol. The camera is slightly to the side. We see Buddy glaring right at Wade. It is dead silent but for the MUSIC on the box. [Image of Wade's power diminished by putting Buddy and stone stare into frame])

BUDDY: You ever shoot anybody was looking you in the eye?

WADE: Who said anything about shootin' anybody?

(Buddy has his gun out under the table. He slowly brings it up and lays it flat on the table, not taking his hand off it or his eyes off Wade. Camera cuts very quickly for a close-up of Wade as he watches the gun come up. His face shows slight concern.)

BUDDY: Whole different story; isn't it?

WADE: You're fired. You're outta the department.

BUDDY: There's not a soul in this county isn't sick to death of your bullshit, Charley. You made yourself scarce, you could make a lot of people happy.

WADE: You little pissant–

BUDDY: Now or later, Charley. You won't have any trouble finding me.

(Wade feels the people around him waiting for a reaction. He leans close to Buddy, face almost right on the camera, to croak in a hoarse whisper.,,

WADE: You're a dead man.

(As Wade and Hollis exit, the camera cuts to a close-up of Buddy with a slight smirk on his face. He speaks in Spanish and orders a beer. He then looks up slightly and the camera follows the angle of his gaze as it pans to Sam standing over the table, listening. We are back in 1995.)

In this one scene, the audience learns:

- the white and Chicano communities are fighting for identity and relevance;

- the identity of the found body;

- Charley Wade's corruption and his mean spirited dangerous nature;

- Buddy Deeds' sense of right and wrong and his cool demeanor and courage; and

- the notion that Buddy might be Wade's killer is heightened.

The first glimpse of a troubled parent-child relationship is also put forth. This is the core scene upon which the rest of the movie is based in both story and filmmaking art.

With few exceptions, close-up shots are primarily used in this scene. In this case, the technique not only brings the audience into the scene but also shows the characters' emotions. There is a very narrow depth of field, so that the backgrounds are blurred and faded, placing greater emphasis on the subjects. The camera angles heighten the tension while also helping to mold the viewer's identification level with the characters. In the same scene, Sayles also reveals his effective technique for flashbacks, which he uses throughout the movie. Instead of cuts or fades, the camera simply pans to a slightly different spot in the immediate area and the past is revealed.

After the flashback is played out, a further pan brings the audience back to the present. This technique helps provide a sense of history of the exact spot; it ties the past and present together both in time and the generation of the characters. Young and older, parent and child. It provides a smooth continuity of story, and, importantly, the technique does not break the viewer's concentration.

Once the badge found at the scene is cleaned up and confirmed, Sam Deeds is pretty sure the body is Charley Wade and suspects that his father, Buddy, who was Charley Wade's deputy and eventually became sheriff, was the killer. Through Sam's investigation, we learn Charley Wade was the absolute personification of a brutal, racist, over-controlling individual who abused his power at every turn. We also learn that Charley would kill for no reason, often tricking blacks and Mexicans into do something that would provide an excuse for him to kill them in cold blood.

One person he killed was Mercedes' husband who was helping some Mexicans into the country. Ironically, this is also how her husband met Mercedes, who is an illegal who crossed the river years earlier. It is ironic because she now insists her employees only speak English and reports illegal immigrants to the border patrol. She portrays a rigid mother, employer, and community member. She looks down at those less fortunate who represent what she once was. Her rigidness and disappointment in her daughter is reflected by a similar rigidness in Del and his insistence that his son adhere to certain standards. We also come to realize that Sam feels he cannot live up to the community's perception of his father or the standards Buddy set in the home.

Throughout the film, the camera often pans over the scenery before the characters are seen. This quickly acclimates the viewer with the location and its purpose. To facilitate the continuity, there is a lot of camera movement, which superbly serves the narration and the film's themes. Many close-ups are from a slight angle rather than head-on. This technique puts the characters into proper perspective in the *mise-en-scène*.

Color is not used just as an accent, but also has meaning within the scene. The building containing the Mexican restaurant is made of orange Mexican brick, while the buildings on either side of it are bright white. Its interior has a lot of orange and blue on the walls. That particular color combination is often considered representative of the hot summer sun and cool refreshing water—perfect for the respite of the restaurant from the outdoors. These colors clearly distinguish that structure from those of the blacks or whites.

Big O's is the black bar and dance hall. It is a dark wooden structure near the desert surrounding the fort. It appears to be in need of repair. The first time we see the interior, it is very dark with a lot of blue and red filtered light that accompanies the blues music heard in the background. The colors convey the party-like atmosphere and escapism, as well as provide a definitive tie-in to the scene and history.

Perhaps the most striking use of color occurs when Sam and his love Pilar are sitting in her mother's Mexican restaurant with most of the lights out. They have gotten together for just the second time since high school and are sitting on two chairs, looking out the window as if sitting on a porch. There is a warm red-orange filter over everything but the bright-white glare of the jukebox. The two of them appear to blend into the room. They dance to *Since I Met You, Baby* sung in Spanish. The orange tint carries over as the scene fades to Sam and Pilar making love in Sam's apartment. Providing an erotic scene from start to finish, once again Sayles provides a soft continuity between the shots.

Those who deal with the psychology of color say that orange radiates warmth and happiness, combining the physical energy and stimulation of red with the cheerfulness of yellow. Orange promotes a sense of general well-being and emotional energy that should be shared, such as compassion, passion, and warmth. It will help a person recover from disappointments, a wounded heart, or a blow to one's pride. Orange is associated with meanings of joy, warmth, change, stimulation, happiness, sexuality, freedom, and expression. Red-orange relates to passion, pleasure, and desire. These descriptions fit the scenes perfectly. It is clear the cinematographer understood the effect of his work and its influence on the viewer.

Lone Star not only focuses on the geographical border between the countries, but also the various borders in relationships and how people cross lines in them by their behaviors. This theme is consistent: Charley Wade crossed the line by accepting bribes and killing those who did not go along with his schemes; Mercedes, who herself is an illegal alien having crossed the river to enter the U.S., now crosses the line to contemptuously report others she sees doing it; even up to the last scene in the film, when Pilar and Sam agree to cross a natural taboo.

A scene occurs about one-third of the way into the film that shows white parents trying to maintain lines, Mexican parents wanting their own lines, and the teachers trying to cross them all to provide what they believe is a balanced point of view.

ANGLO MOTHER: You're just tearin' everything down! Tearin' down our heritage, tearin' down the memory of people that fought and died for this land.

CHICANO FATHER: (Off Screen.) We fought and died for this land, too!

WHIP PAN see another Chicano--

CHICANO FATHER: We fought the U.S. Army, the Texas Rangers--

ANGLO FATHER: (Off Screen.) Yeah, but you lost, buddy!

WHIP PAN to a man in the rear--

ANGLO FATHER: Winners get the bragging rights, that's how it goes.

PRINCIPAL: People--people--

(PULL OUT WIDER: We see a group of parents sitting around a small room some on chairs at a table others on the perimeter on the backs of the chairs or sitting on a table. Pilar and another teacher sit at the end of a long table facing the agitated parents, taking some heat.

DANNY PADILLA, a young, Chicano reporter, sits in the corner taking notes, enjoying the show.)

PRINCIPAL (C.U.): I think it would be best not to put things in terms of winners and losers–

ANGLO MOTHER (C.U.) (Points at Pilar): Well, the way she's teachin' it has got everything switched around. I was on the textbook committee, and her version is not--

PRINCIPAL: We think of the textbook as kind of a guide, not an absolute--

ANGLO MOTHER: --it is not what we set as the standard! Now you people can believe what you want, but when it comes to teaching our children--

CHICANO MOTHER: They're our children, too! (PAN to show this mother.)

Pan to ANGLO FATHER: The men who founded this state have a right to have their story–

PULL OUT TO DANNY TALKING DIRECTLY TO THE
ANGLO FATHER: The men who founded this state broke
from Mexico because they needed   slavery to be legal
to make a fortune in the cotton business!

PILAR: I think that's a bit of an oversimplification--

ANGLO FATHER: Are you reporting this meeting or
runnin' it, Danny?

DANNY: Just adding a little historical perspective--

ANGLO FATHER: (Starts talking off screen as camera pans
toward him) You may call it history, but I call it propagan-
da. I'm sure they got their own account of the Alamo on
the other side, but we're not on the other side, so we're not
about to have it taught in our schools!

PILAR: There's no reason to be so threatened by this--

(Pilar is trying to stay calm despite her anger.)

PILAR: I've only been trying to get across some of the
complexity of our situation down here--cultures coming
together in both negative and positive ways.

ANGLO MOTHER: If you mean like music and food and
all, I have no problem with that.

(REVERSE. We shoot towards Pilar as her daughter
PALOMA steps up to whisper to her.)

ANGLO MOTHER: --but when you start changing who
did what to who.

WHITE TEACHER: We're not changing anything, we're
presenting a more complete picture.

ANGLO MOTHER: And that's what's got to stop!

(Pilar looks troubled by what she's heard. She shoots a
look toward the others at the table, then slips away with
Paloma–)

TEACHER: There's enough ignorance in the world
without us encouraging it in the classroom--

ANGLO MOTHER: Now who are you calling ignorant?

PRINCIPAL: Folks, I know this is a very emotional issue for
some of you, but we do have other business to attend to--

It is unusual for a script to have the shooting instructions
in it as you see in this previous excerpt. In this case, since
Sayles was the writer, director, and editor, he was able to
create a shooting script early in the process. The camera
whips back and forth to each of the speakers, giving the
audience a realistic feeling of the intensity of their fears and

anger in the meeting and the pace of events. The camera work aids in giving the dialogue the right effect.

One of the themes conveyed (by combining several scenes) was the effects of divorce. The first scene is at Del's home where we learn he is O's son, and he refuses to meet him. O left the family when Del was young for another woman down the street and never had any contact with them. Del's anger and hatred are seen in full force. A little later, we see Del's son, Chet, going to Big O's bar to see his grandfather. He carries O's picture with him since he has never seen him. We learn that, unlike his father, Chet would very much like a relationship with his grandfather. He needs some support and relief from his strict disciplinarian father.

Later in the film, after a young black female soldier helped Del look at life a little differently, he visits his father's home. O is not at home, but his current wife shows Del around the house. Suddenly Del sees a display of framed articles about him as he grew up and his career in the service. He asks her how O got them, and the wife tells him that Del's uncle sent them. Del comments that his mother had said his father never asked about him, to which the wife responds, "He never asked her." At Chet's urging, Del finally agrees to invite his father over for barbeque. This theme is developed over time within the movie. The viewer must put the various scenes together to discern the real meaning being conveyed by the filmmaker.

The name Buddy Deeds appears to have significant meaning. Folks in town are constantly talking about how much a person could rely on Buddy if they needed anything and how he did more for the town than anyone.

Hence, he is a "buddy" to many people. His "deeds" were often admirable, while others were self-serving. He didn't take bribe money, but he was just as corrupt as Charley Wade was in how he did business. It was the way people perceived him that made the difference. Charley was seen as a bully, and Buddy was considered helpful.

In the next-to-the-last scene, the mystery of the killer is solved. The flashback shows Charley Wade being shot just as he was getting ready to kill another minority he had tricked into putting a gun in his hand. Shots ring out, and Charley's blood shoots out over the "blood money" he was at the bar to collect: a sign of his corruption and justice being delivered in a minority bar.

The film could have easily ended with the solving of the mystery. But Sayles adds one more scene at the remains of a drive-in. As teenagers, Sam and Pilar were at the drive-in when Buddy discovered them together and immediately split them apart. They were never allowed to date again, and did not talk to each other until a few days before this scene takes place. On its face, the drive-in is a fitting place to say good-bye to the past and renew their relationship. But Sayles throws in an extra punch. Sam discloses Buddy's affair with Mercedes and the fact that he and Pilar are half siblings. Pilar emphasizes that she can no longer have children, making it clear she loves him and wants to continue their life together. Sam agrees.

SAM: If I met you for the first time today, I'd still want to be with you.

(It is what Pilar needed to hear—)

PILAR: We start from scratch--

SAM: Yeah--

PILAR: Everything that went before, all that stuff, that history--the hell with it, right?

(PILAR takes Sam's hand, kisses him--)

PILAR: Forget the Alamo.

(WIDE SHOT, DRIVE-IN. Sam and Pilar sit by each other holding hands, looking at the empty screen--)

MUSIC, ROLL CREDITS

So instead of walking out with the fun of finally learning how Charley died, the audience is left to mull over a scene about hope, love, and looking toward the future and decide if the scene's incestuous nature taints it. Keeps you thinking all the way home and beyond.

TELL NO ONE
[NE LE DIS À PERSONNE] (2006)

- Directed by Guillaume Canet
- Screenplay by Guillaume Canet, adapted from the novel by Harlan Cohen
- Edited by Herve de Luze
- Distributed by *Les Productions du Trésor* and EuropaCorp
- USA distributor: Music Box Films, Sony Classic Pictures

Françoise Cluzet – Publicity still Music Box Films (2006)

PRIMARY CHARACTERS:

- Alex Beck: A pediatrician whose wife was killed eight years ago, but has suddenly become a suspect again.
- Margot Beck: Alex's wife

- Jacques Laurentin: Margot's father
- Anne Beck: Alex's sister
- Hélène Perkins: Anne's wife
- Eric Levkowitch: Investigating police officer
- Bruno: A gangster Alex once helped and who is now returning the favor.

FROM THE CRITICS:

Roger Ebert in *Chicago Sun Times*, **July 10, 2008:**

"*Tell No One* will play as a terrific thriller for you, if you meet it halfway. You have to be willing to believe. There will be times you think it's too perplexing, when you're sure you're witnessing loose ends. It has been devised that way, and the director knows what he's doing. Even when it's baffling, it's never boring. I've heard of airtight plots. This one is not merely airtight, but hermetically sealed."

In his review, Roger Ebert provided a perfect non-disclosing description of the film:

"It contains a rich population of characters, but has been so carefully cast that we're never confused. There are: Alex's sister; her lesbian lover; the rich senator, whose obsession is horses; Margot's father; the police captain who alone believes Alex is innocent; the helpful crook, and the senator's son (played by director Canet himself). Also a soft-porn fashion photographer, a band of vicious assassins, street thugs, and on and on. And the movie gives full weight to these characters; they are necessary and handled with care.

One of the film's pleasures is its unexpected details. The big dog Alex hauls around. The Christian Louboutin red-soled shoes that are worn on two most unlikely occasions. The steeplechase right in the middle of everything. The way flashbacks are manipulated in their framing so that the first one shows less than when it is reprised. The way solutions are dangled before us and then jerked away. The computer technique. The torturous path taken by some morgue photos. The seedy lawyer, so broke his name is scrawled on cardboard taped to the door. Alex patiently tutoring a young child. That the film clocks at only a whisper above two hours is a miracle."

Stephen Holden in the New York Times, July 2, 2008:

v"Guillaume Canet's delicious contemporary thriller *Tell No One* is *Vertigo* meets *The Fugitive* by way of *The Big Sleep*. That is meant as high praise. . ..The story, which involves murder and depravity in high places, is so elaborately twisty that about halfway through the movie you stop trying to figure it out and let its polluted waters wash over you, trusting that the denouement will reveal all. It does and it doesn't."

Kirk Honeycutt in the *Hollywood Reporter*, April 22, 2007:

"Hardly anyone can make a good old American suspense thriller like the French."

SYNOPSIS

An innocent man is on the run after he's accused of murder and his spouse, seemingly, returns from the grave in this thriller from France. Alex Beck is a doctor who has slowly been putting his life back together after his wife,

Margot, was murdered by a serial killer. Eight years later, Alex is doing well enough until he finds himself implicated in the murder of two people, and there is plenty of evidence pointing to him as the killer even though he knows nothing of the crimes.

The same day, Alex receives an e-mail that appears to be from Margot, which includes a link to an apparently recent video clip that features his late wife looking alive and well. Margot's message warns Alex that they are both being watched, and he struggles to stay one step ahead of the law as a gang of strong-arm men intimidate Alex's friends into telling whatever they might know about him. Alex's sister Anne persuades her well-to-do wife to hire respected attorney Elisabeth Feldman to handle Alex's case. While Elisabeth tries to keep Alex out of jail, she learns that there is a warrant out for her client's arrest; Alex goes on the lam while they struggle to learn the truth about the murder as well as Margot's reappearance. *Tell No One* (aka *Ne le Dis à Personne*) was based on the international best-selling novel by Harlan Coben.

ANALYSIS

Tell No One is a mystery thriller that requires viewers to use of all of Münsterberg's processes (perception, attention, memory, imagination, suggestion, and emotions) while viewing. There are a number of things in the beginning of the film the viewer has no reason to pay particular attention to at the time they are seen or heard. Over an hour later in the film, though, the ability to recall these things on the fly will provide definite clues to unraveling the mystery.

Alex is married to Margot, and they are very much in love. She is killed, and he has never gotten over her loss. The police believed he was guilty, but eventually arrested and convicted a serial killer. Eight years later, two bodies are dug up, and one of them has a key to Margot's secret lockbox, leading the police to begin questioning Alex again.

Right before Margot's death, she and Alex had been swimming in a private lake, when she swam ashore and then cried out. Alex swam to see what was happening and, as he climbed out of the water, he was knocked back into the water unconscious. Police have always wondered how he got back on land since that is where he was found in a coma.

Then a series of subplots begin that put Alex back as a prime suspect and also in grave danger. One subplot involves the fact that he has received two mysterious e-mails that can only be opened by somebody who understands the times described, and that person is Alex. These e-mails imply Margot is still alive.

There is only one way to eventually understand and enjoy this film: viewers must sit back and let themselves be carried, as if on a magic carpet, through the labyrinth of subplots, chases, deception, and unveilings. Pay close attention to everything presented on-screen, ride the emotional roller coaster, and put your memory to work—because nothing in the first two acts discloses or hints at what really happened before, during, and after Margot's death/disappearance. The audience becomes ensnarled by the tension and emotions, the cutting back and forth to a number of stories, and the superbly casted acting. This movie's flashbacks often contain further flashbacks and, at times, keep going back and forth in a montage style.

Some believe one of the film's themes is a commentary on the French justice system due to the fact that several clues leading to this conclusion are interwoven throughout the film:

1. When Alex was discovered on the edge of the lake where Margot was killed, he is unconscious and remains in a coma in the hospital for days. The police still have him as their prime suspect until a serial murderer is caught. The clues at Margot's murder scene appeared to match this man's *modus operendi*, and he is charged, although it is the one murder he does not admit to committing.

2. Bruno has a young hemophiliac son, and Alex treated the boy early in his childhood, preventing Bruno from being charged with child battery. When the man comes back several years later with the boy in bad shape, he will not let any other doctor treat the child because they were already calling child welfare. Again Alex saves the day.

3. In the new investigation of Alex, there is a bad cop/good cop scenario. One of the investigating officers does not believe Alex is guilty and, at one point, tips off Alex's attorney that police are going to arrest him. This officer determines, through

thorough police work, that the body found at the
scene was not Margot.

4. Alex is framed to look like he killed a friend of
    Margot's during the second investigation. Only the
    one police officer is unsure of Alex's guilt, while
    others jump to conclusions without sufficient
    evidence.

5. Finally, Margot's father tells Alex about sex crimes,
    corruption, and murder that occurred, which he
    kept quiet about because he was on the take. He
    describes how other officers and judicial officers
    were also on the take.

All of these things come out in the midst of some other
story and are part of the constantly changing focal point,
keeping the viewer's mind constantly active.

A truly beautiful but sad montage begins with Alex
daydreaming about Margot's funeral: it shows the coffin
being carried into the cremation box, then flashes to
their wedding, and then to the two of them as very young
children playing in the lake. We see them approaching a
tree in which they have carved a heart with their initials and
added a notch for each year. Back to a scene of the deck at
the lake. Back to the flames exploding out at the coffin. The
camera isolates a friend or family member at each event,
first showing them smiling and happy and then in dressed
in black and crying. The viewer cannot help but feel both

joy and loss and gets pulled into Alex's world. The song *Lilac Wine* is being sung in the background throughout all of this:

I drink much more that I ought to drink

Because it brings me back you

Lilac wine is sweet and heady, like my love

Lilac wine, I feel unsteady, like my love

Listen to me, I cannot see clearly

Isn't that she, coming to me nearly here?

Lilac wine is sweet and heady where's my love?

Lilac wine, I feel unsteady, where's my love?

Listen to me, why is everything so hazy?

Isn't that she, or am I just going crazy, dear?

In this film, song lyrics are as important as dialogue; they tell the emotional part of the story. The music used matches the scene: melancholy songs evoke thoughts of romance and then loss, while other scenes have pulsating music to help build tension and excitement.

The cinematography is also an important storytelling element. There are a number of long shots building the introduction to some scenes. One is a helicopter shot that provides a view high above the beautiful full-color countryside and the road on which Alex and Margot are driving. An idyllic day.

Most of the shots in the film are medium to medium close to keep the viewer as an observer, yet close enough to feel the tension. A few close-ups show the actors' emotions at key times. The combinations and frequent changes keep the intense pace right in the viewer's seat. The warm, rose-colored hues of the outdoor scenery around the home and lake set up the love and then the loss.

An interesting angle and subject reversal early in the film provides room for interpretation. As Alex and Margo drive from the family house to the lake, the camera is high above them. A little later, after dark, Alex is lying on a raft in the middle of the lake as Margot swims ashore. The camera looks up into the sky from his position, showing the stars on a clear night. Is this to represent love or loss? Although there are a few long set-up shots, the majority are close-ups or middle close. This keeps the viewer as an active observer, often feeling "in" the shot. The lighting used also constantly conveys emotion and meaning. From bright, colorful light to dark shadows, the lighting is an active contributor to the roller-coaster labyrinth the viewer is taken to. There are very subtle changes and coloring, but each shot is distinctive.

Earlier I mentioned how things seen at the beginning come into play at the end. Right after a family picnic, Alexandre and Margot go to a lake and walk through a curving path of rhododendrons on their way to carve another notch into their heart on a tree. Toward the end of the film, Alex is standing outside his sister's apartment, talking with a police officer, when someone walks up to the door carrying a basket of rhododendrons and tells the maid that they are for Alexandre Beck. The camera pans back to Alex's face, and it is clear he understands what they represent. We never see what is written on the card that came with them. The next day Margot's father discloses what actually happened at the lake eight years ago. Alex immediately drives back to the lake. He again walks down the path of flowers to the tree and finds eight brand-new notches have been added. He immediately falls to the ground, crying as he hears a rustling behind him and Margot walks up to take him in her arms. Alex knew Margot was definitely alive the moment the rhododendrons were delivered.

One of the clues the audience only sees as it occurs is when one of the e-mails Alex receives is from "M&A" followed by a bunch of forward slashes (/). It tells him to go to a URL link at a particular time and use the ID: "Concert" and password: "Olympia." He follows the instructions, but cannot open the site. He then takes the dog for a walk in the park and sits, pondering. Suddenly, he jumps up and starts running. As he runs, we hear U2 singing the song *With or Without You* in the background. It keeps playing as Alex gets to his computer and enters "U2" instead of "Concert" and "1995" instead of "Olympia". The message opens. The clue would only have meant something to Alex and Margot, but it reaffirms his belief that Margot is alive. "M&A" obviously means Margot and Alex, and if we had counted the forward slashes (/) in the header, it would have added up to the number of years Margot and Alex had loved each other, matching the notches on the tree plus eight.

It is only after *Tell No One* is over and you exhale and begin to breathe, that you can begin to sift through and look for meaning. Was the film offering political comment on the French justice system? Why would Margot go eight years without her husband who she loved dearly—or was it that dearly? Like *Lone Star*, the film does contain issues about morality, corruption, violence, love, and family problems. But it is all conveyed so differently and with subtlety. This film is truly one that cries out for a second viewing.

AMOUR (2012)

- Written and directed by Michael Haneke
- Edited by Nadine Muse and Monika Willi
- Distributed by *Les Films du Losange*, X-Filme Creative Pool, Wega Film
- USA distributor: Sony Picture Classics

Director Michael Haneke with Costars Emmanuelle Riva and Jean-Louis Trintignant--Sony/Photofest

PRIMARY CHARACTERS:

- George and Anne Laurent: Husband and wife; former piano teachers
- Eva: Their married daughter

FROM THE CRITICS:

Philip French in *The Guardian*, **November 17, 2012:**

"*Amour* will, I believe, take its place alongside the greatest films about the confrontation of ageing and death, among them Ozu's *Tokyo Story*, Kurosawa's *Living*, Bergman's *Wild Strawberries*, Rosi's *Three Brothers* and, dare I say it, Don Siegel's *The Shootist*."

SYNOPSIS

An octogenarian couple find their love put to the ultimate test when one suffers a stroke, and the other must assume the caretaker role in this compassionate yet unsentimental drama. Two retired classical music teachers are savoring their golden years in a comfortable apartment, when the wife, Anne, experiences a stroke that leaves her partially paralyzed. Her devoted husband, George, struggles with the formidable task of being Anne's full-time caretaker. A visit from their adult daughter Eva reaffirms just how secluded from society the highly educated couple have become. The movie concludes with an ultimate, moralistic test of their caring.

ANALYSIS

The themes in this film are simple and straight forward: love and devotion; aging, elderly debility, and dementia and their effects upon the person and his or her family; mercy killing; and death. After the opening, these themes are presented in a strictly linear, unencumbered manner.

The opening scene essentially prepares viewers for how the film will end. The film opens with the fire department breaking down the front door of an apartment. We see this from inside the apartment as if we were standing there, waiting for it to happen, and saying, *It's time you showed up for my story*. The camera then follows one of the firemen around the apartment. We see him encounter a terrible smell and is forced to open the windows. Within moments, we learn it is the stench of death as another door is opened, and we see a female corpse all laid out with dying flowers spread around her.

Cut to the flashback, and the journey begins. The scene is a wide shot of a concert hall. The camera is on the stage, looking out at the audience that awaits the start of a piano recital. Typical of Haneke's approach, nothing directs our attention to anyone in particular. One couple rises to let a man pass by to his seat, so it does not seem special. They are, however, our subject characters. As we hear the opening strains of Schubert's *Impromptu Opus No. 1*, the woman closes her eyes and just listens. The music sets a tone of soothing elegance: slightly formal, but still with a lively lilt. This pattern of musical use continues throughout most of the film. It complements the image of the couple who act in a slightly formal manner, but still full of life for each other.

The couple, George and Anne Laurent, are played by French cinematic icons Emmanuelle Riva and Jean-Louis Trintignant, who are both now in their 80s. These two stars assume their roles as if they had worn them all of their lives. Another strong performance in the film is given by Isabelle Huppert, who plays their somewhat removed daughter, Eva. Never does the viewer believe they are watching actors. We are, indeed, observers, but are granted sufficient entry via the camera to be intimate observers.

When they return from the concert, George and Anne discover that someone has attempted to break into their apartment. We see our first of many indications of caring, when George calms Anne by saying, "Don't let it spoil your good mood now." He then, as a gentleman, helps her take her coat off. When she goes into the bedroom to change he says, "Did I tell you, you looked good tonight?"

The next morning during breakfast, Anne suffers an episode that leaves her immobile, staring straight into space. This scene has the first close-up shots of the movie. It is this scene that provides an even deeper look at George's love and caring; not only is there shock and fear reflected in his face, but also love. He is close to tears when she does not respond to him. At the same time, his controlled, steady manner as he attempts to revive her provides the first glimpse into his strength. As he is preparing to get help, she appears to recover. They argue over whether to call a doctor, but she cannot remember anything that has happened.

We then meet their daughter, Eva. She and her father are in the living room talking about her life. There are warm, rich colors in the furniture, clothing, and lighting. The walls are covered with bookshelves and pictures. It is a cozy, warm, secure atmosphere, but also a very traditional room that conveys Anne and George's generation. Finally, Eva asks about her mother, and we learn Anne has had an operation for a blocked artery, and it failed. More strokes can be expected, and she will get progressively worse. Some meaningful lines from both George and Eva follow. Eva asks how she can help, and George responds:

GEORGE: No, really. There's nothing you can do. We'll see how things go when she's back here in the apartment.

We'll manage. Maybe I'll get a caretaker in, or maybe I'll manage on my own. We'll see. We've been through quite a lot in our time, your mother and I.

(little laugh)

All this is still a bit new."

PAUSE.

EVA (with a little laugh): It's funny. I don't know if I should say it. Maybe it'll embarrass you. But when I came here a short while ago, I suddenly remembered how I always used to listen to the two of you making love when I was little. For me, at the time, it was reassuring. It gave me a feeling that you loved each other, and that we'd always be together.

George is talking about the closeness of their marriage, and Eva conveys how her parents love provided a sense of security. It is a little uncomfortable hearing a daughter talk about her parents' lovemaking, but it draws the viewer into the character's shoes.

There is a cut to sometime in the future as the apartment door opens. Again we, the viewers, are inside the apartment, greeting them as George enters followed by a paramedic who wheels Anne in a wheelchair. George is very unsettled and not sure how to act. After they settle in the living room, Anne makes George promise that he will never take her back to the hospital. There is no discussion allowed. This is her wish, and he is to follow it.

After helping Anne into bed, George hovers over her, unsure of what else he can do to help. The bedroom has shades of yellow and a warm glow. Light comes primarily from table lamps, creating shadows. Anne is obviously worried about George and tries to reassure him that she can do things for herself. She is suppressing her fear of what is to come the best she can.

By now the director has used the placement of the camera, close-up shots, and warm lighting and colors to make the viewer feel comfortably at home and use their point of view to be an integral part of the story. One slowly realizes why the shots of people coming into the apartment are always from the inside. Some might interpret it as having the audience "share" the apartment with the characters. I do not believe that is the case. Rather, I believe the entire movie is shot from the *point of view* of the apartment itself. The one scene that convinces me of the latter is the last scene when Eva returns to the apartment after both of her parents are dead. The camera is still inside and follows her around as she walks through the apartment.

A scene that begins to convey the humiliation of Anne's inability to care for herself shows George waiting outside the bathroom. She calls for him to come in, and she is seen on the toilet with her panties below her knees. He helps her stand and then pulls her panties up for her, just like one would do for a toddler. This is a medium-long shot so that the viewer is not intrusive but present. Despite George's gentleness, it is a brutal shot for the audience. It evokes sadness, pity, and the fear that we could end up that way.

The next day, they are sitting at the kitchen table, and George tells Anne a story describing what is discussed in this book. It is about a time when he was young and went to a movie alone. Leaving the movie theater, George found himself to be very emotional, but he was fine by the time he got home. A short time later, he recounted the film to a neighbor and became even more emotional than when he was leaving the theater. What he described was that as we relax and let ourselves absorb what we have seen, the more a film will have meaning for us. However, I do not believe that is why this story was in this film. Rather, it was a way for George to describe how his emotions were playing upon him in the present without directly admitting it.

As the movie progresses and Anne's condition deteriorates, several things happen. George looks older and older. His skin begins to wrinkle even more, then starts appearing shriveled. He begins to look nearly as gaunt as Anne, because he, too, is slowly fading. Accompanying this, the lighting of the scenes initially darkens slowly, and then it becomes brighter, but harsher and colder. The characters faces become almost devoid of color. This lighting conveys not only the changes in Anne's condition, but what is happening in their relationship. After Anne's death, George is found writing a letter in very dark room with only the light of a small table lamp shining on the letter.

When Anne is unable to speak, she communicates with her eyes, and George starts responding in a like manner. The audience has no trouble understanding the communication and can identify with both of them. All of this is quite effective in carrying the viewer through the time span. It helps you feel their lives slowly fading out. Interestingly, however, the lighting never becomes really cold until we see the apartment when Eva comes back to the house after her parents' deaths.

At various times throughout the film, we see George's embarrassment at having to talk about Anne's condition with others. It is up to the viewer's interpretation as to whether he is embarrassed for himself or for Anne. We get some answers much later in the film when Eva visits George again:

> ". . .[J]ust to explain why I didn't answer your phone calls and why I don't want to have any pointless discussions on the subject. Your mother is just as could have been expected: bad the whole time.
>
> She is turning more and more into a helpless child, and it's sad and humiliating, for her and for me. And she doesn't want to be seen in that state either. Even the last time you visited, she didn't want you to come. You two have your own life. Nothing wrong with that. But let us have our life too. Even though it's a lousy one. OK?
>
> We do our speech exercises every day, or we sing together. Most of the time, I wake up around 5. At that time, she's still awake. Then we change her incontinence pad. I rub cream on her to avoid sores. Then, around 7, I try to persuade her to eat and drink. Sometimes it works, sometimes not.

Sometimes she tells me things from her childhood, then for hours she calls for help, and then an instant later she's giggling away to herself, or crying. Nothing of any of that deserves to be shown."
And it is not shown in the film.

In the process of caring for Anne, George has blocked Eva out. He won't answer her calls or return them when she leaves a message. He tells Eva, almost angrily, "Your concern is of no use to me. I don't have time to deal with your concern, that's all." We see the pain and disappointment on Eva's face and begin to feel the emotion of isolation. During that last soliloquy, the camera focuses on Eva's face, and we see her begin to realize just how bad things are and what is coming. She looks worn and sad.

As the film progresses, George is being forced to watch the person he has loved and lived with for over fifty years lose not only her physical and mental capabilities, but her very existence, her identity. Their love is slowly being dismantled along with his life. He does not want to see Anne this way, and he does not want to remember her this way, and his anger grows. The beginning of this attitude is seen at one point about half way through the movie: Anne has regressed to where she is now rambling incoherently and requiring a lot more physical assistance, and we are shown a scene that starts with Anne playing the piano. She looks elegant and beautiful. The camera pans to George watching her, and then he turns and forcefully stops the CD player. He is already trying to remember her as she once was.

One day George comes home to find Anne on the floor and all the lights out. She has not been able to get back into her wheelchair. Once he gets her into bed, she tells him there is no sense to keep going, no reason to inflict herself upon him. "I do not want to go on," she says, and it is left to the audience to decide if Anne is talking about committing suicide, assisted suicide, or something else.

A little later in the movie though, Anne and George are sitting at the dinner table and she insists on seeing their photo albums immediately. As she goes through them, she comments on how beautiful life is—and so long. George stares at her with a worried look on his face. She tells him to stop staring and, "I'm not that stupid, yet." Later in the film, Anne has deteriorated even more. She has to be spoon-fed soft food, drinks out of a toddler bottle, and one time soils herself in bed. The scene shows her unable to talk, and George tries to give her water that she does not want it. He says, "If you don't drink, you'll die. Do you want that?" The look she gives him clearly says, *Obviously, fool.* But George keeps trying to force her and threatens to take her back to the hospital. The anger in her face is very clear. She spits out the water, too weak to spit on George. He slaps her. The camera goes back and forth on each of their faces as they both realize how bad things have gotten. Neither can look at the other. The silence is very emotional for the viewer. Then the director uses a strange cut to a series of paintings, none of which seem to have any relationship to what has just occurred in the film.

Haneke's style of not filling in explanations for the audience is, while intellectually challenging, also extremely frustrating. Often there is little background or in the *mise-en-scène* to guide us. In a post screening discussion at the film's debut, the director was asked if the paintings meant anything specific or if it was simply open to the audience's interpretation.

Haneke answered: "It's open to interpretation. All the things you mentioned—not just the paintings but also the pigeons, for example, and any number of other elements—are open to interpretation. In fact, that's why they're in the film to confront the audience, to invite the audience to think about these questions. For that reason, it would be counterproductive if I were to impose a specific, rigid, single meaning on those elements. If I tell the audience what they should think, then I am robbing them of their own imagination and their own capacity of deciding what's important to them. That scene was one of the emotional climaxes of the film, and that's why it's followed by the shots of the paintings, because it would have been impossible to follow simply with a continuation of the story."

Late in the film, George is in the bathroom brushing his teeth when the doorbell rings. He opens it but finds nobody there. He then goes exploring down the hallways of the building until he stops and notices that he is standing in several inches of water over his ankles. As he begins to panic, a hand suddenly shoots out from behind his head and covers his mouth. We hear him scream, and there is a cut to show George in bed awakening from his nightmare. There is never any discussion of this dream nor is any other insight inferentially provided. The audience is left to wade through on their own.

After George has killed Anne, we see him struggle to get up from a couch in another room. He goes to the kitchen where Anne is washing the dishes, and she tells him she is almost done so he can put his shoes on if he wants. He helps her with her coat and starts to leave with her. She tells him to get a coat. He does and they walk out of the apartment together. We never learn what happens to George. The next scene shows Eva returning to an empty apartment. Certainly the scenes can be interpreted as George joining Anne in death—but was his a natural death or suicide?

The scene when Eva returns to the apartment, as usual finds the camera inside as she opens the door. Now the director is using long shots of the rooms. We are not intimate with Eva like we were with her parents. She walks around slowly looking at various things and sits down in the living room. Haneke wants the audience to decide if she is trying to contemplate what happened or if she is remembering the loving life she knows occurred in that place.

THE BOOK THIEF (2013)

- Directed by Brian Percival
- Screenplay by Michael Petroni based on the novel by Markus Zusak
- Edited by John Wilson
- Distributed by Fox 2000 Pictures, Sunswept Entertainment, TSG Entertainment

Liesel Meminger played by Sophie Nélise- Publicity Still-Fox Pictures

PRIMARY CHARACTERS:

- Death: An invisible narrator
- Liesel Meminger: A preteen girl
- Hans and Rosa Huberman: Liesel's foster parents
- Rudy Steiner: Liesel's classmate and good friend
- Max Vandenburg: A young Jewish man taken in by the Hubermans
- Ilsa Hermann: The burgermeister's wife

FROM THE CRITICS:

Richard Roeper in the *Chicago Sun Times*,
November 7, 2013:

"This is one of the best movies of the year, featuring one of the most perfect endings of any movie in recent memory.

SYNOPSIS

While placed in a foster home and subjected to the horrors of World War II Germany, an extraordinary, spirited young girl, Liesel, finds solace by stealing books and sharing the stories with others. With the help of her foster parents and a secret guest under the stairs, who is being sheltered by the family, she learns to read and creates a magical world that inspires them all.

ANALYSIS

Before getting into what kind of movie *The Book Thief* is, let's be clear about what it is not. *The Book Thief* is not a Holocaust story. It was never intended to be such by the book's author. In adapting the book to film, the screenwriter never attempted to make it about the Holocaust, and the director was just as clear in his direction. It is a film with a story that takes place during the Holocaust, but it is focused primarily on the non-Jewish Germans.

So what are the themes of this wonderful film? One theme is what life was like in Nazi Germany for a.) ordinary small-town Germans who didn't believe in the movement; and b.) those who chose to join the party out of fear. Secondly, it is a coming-of-age tale about a young girl placed with a foster family by her communist mother in order to save her—even though they originally wanted to collect money to take care of two children. The film helps us understand the impact zealous national socialists have on down-to-earth, normal people outside of the big cities. We are asked to try and understand their dilemmas even if they were the enemy at the time. Finally, it is the story of a very smart young girl, living in a deadly time, and her almost insatiable quest for words and literature.

The story is narrated by a male voice that never identifies itself, but drops sufficient hints so we know it is Death. The narration is a combination of solemn, philosophical explanations and wry, somewhat sardonic humor at times. From Death's perspective, the entire story is a flashback, but it is told in strictly linear manner, and no flashbacks are used. Once during the film we see the back of a man in an overcoat and hat walking down a dark street. We are led to believe that this is Death—it is the only time the narrator appears on the screen.

The lighting and the music (which is used sparingly) set the tones of the scenes. Although important, they are, however, subtle and with few exceptions do not grab the viewer's attention. The music tries to convey the life happening on the screen. In the family's home, the lighting has an orange-yellow tint to it, coming mostly from the side, either through a window or from small table lamps. This helps create two effects: the events took place a long time ago, and there was very little light in these people's lives. Contrast this with the lighting of the burgermeister's home. When we first see the outside of the majestic mansion, it is in bright sunshine, and the trees are in bloom. Inside the lights are bright, enlivening entire rooms. There is still a slight tint to convey that we are still back in time, but the overall message is that we are in an upper class, free home.

Another pointed use of lighting occurs at an outdoor book burning. A number of men in Nazi uniform are on a platform, including the burgermeister, who is addressing the crowd. The lighting on this group is from the ground up onto their faces. The crowd itself is barely lit and the book burning has very bright, intense flames soaring up. This all serves to create an atmosphere of fear and evil. The *mise-en-scène* aptly conveys that the government is controlling the people's freedom.

The theme of the importance of words and literature begins when Liesel's brother is buried early in the film before she is placed in foster care. One of the gravediggers drops a book, and Liesel impulsively picks it up and takes it with her. There is a shot of the book dropping that does not become significant until later in the film. The book falls on some smoldering ashes from a small fire that had been built to keep the people warm. Once at her foster home, Liesel keeps the book close by her even though she cannot read it. A picture of her brother is tucked inside it. When Hans sees the book, he asks if it is hers. Liesel says, "It wasn't always mine." Hans finds out that Liesel cannot read so he agrees to teach her. They read together each night, and by the end of the book she is reading most of it. Hans then takes her down to the basement where he has painted the alphabet around the walls and under each letter he has written words that Liesel had difficulty pronouncing or did not know the meaning. He provides her with chalk and tells her to add whatever words she wants anytime.

When they go to the town's book burning, Liesel gets upset when the burgermeister says that they want to rid Germany of communists. This reinforces her belief that her mother is in trouble. After the rally, Liesel returns to retrieve a book from the smoldering ashes. The burgermeister's wife sees her pick up the book and hide it, but does not give her away. This is an obvious tie back to when she obtained her first book from the ashes. In mythology, a phoenix obtains new life by arising from the ashes of its predecessor. Here the books get new life with a new owner who will gain from reading their words. Similarly, Liesel gets carried into a new life as she becomes educated and learns about life from the stories she reads.

When the young Jewish man, Max, arrives at the Hubermans' he is carrying a copy of *Mein Kampf*, which he's been using to make the police believe he is a Nazi party member. When Liesel asks if it is his, he replies, "It wasn't always mine." This helps set up a bond between the two. One day Rosa sends Liesel to the burgermeister's house to deliver laundry. His wife, Ilsa Hermann, takes Liesel into a library filled with books. Liesel's eyes twinkle as a piano makes the sound of twinkling in the background. She is allowed to take one book and read it there. Liesel learns that the library was Ilsa's son's, but he is missing in action in the war. Ilsa tells Liesel that she may come back and read any time, so she starts memorizing the stories and taking words back to put on the alphabet wall. One day they are caught by the burgermeister, and Liesel is banished from the mansion.

Liesel is hooked, though, and she starts sneaking back into the library through the window. She starts "borrowing" books. On one trip Liesel looks back and sees Ilsa watching her from the window, but knows that Ilsa approves. She is attracted to Liesel because her missing son also loved books, and the library is mostly his books. Having Liesel there helps Ilsa deal with her loss. Liesel uses the books, in part, as a remembrance of her own loss. She keeps a picture of her brother in one of the books. Later in life Liesel uses her writing, her words, to express her losses, her life, and her growth.

Because he is forced to stay in the basement to evade Nazi capture, Max has Liesel describe the outside and what she does every day. She must not only tell him the weather term, but describe it so that Max can picture it and experience it through her words. Liesel also starts telling Max the stories she has memorized. He quotes Aristotle: "Memory is the scribe of the soul." For a Christmas present, Max painted all the *Mein Kampf* pages white so Liesel can use it as a diary. He has written the Hebrew word for "write" in it and tells her that his religion believes that every living thing "is only alive because it contains the secret word for life. That's the only difference between us and a lump of clay. A word. Words are life, Liesel. All those blank pages... they're for you to fill."

Composer John Williams, who wrote the score for the film, says that what he took away from the story was: "Words can save you. Words can offer solace to you. Words can offer immortality to you."

During an air raid Liesel tries to calm the people by telling them one of the stories she had memorized. They were thankful. Later, when Hans returns from the war, he and Liesel are talking:

HANS: Your mama told me what you did.

LIESEL: I shouldn't have.

HANS: Maybe you had to.

LIESEL: I keep thinking about Max. Wondering where he is.

HANS: Me, too. What he went through. Everything we did.

LIESEL: We were just being people. That's what people do.

HANS: I'm not sure what it all meant.

LIESEL: Everything

HANS: Liesel. . .you are all grown up.

This conversation ties the value of words theme with that of how people treat each other.

And, lastly, Liesel survives when everyone else is killed during an accidental bombing of the town because she was in the basement writing in her diary and had fallen asleep.

In the closing scene, we learn from Death, that Liesel became a famous writer and published many books.

Another theme concerns how people treat each other. We see both the good and the bad. Scenes that reflect the bad include:

1.   the mistreatment of Jews, one of which, interestingly, was not in this town;

2.   the talk and actions of a mean bully in Liesel's class who always puts others down due to his own inferiority problems;

3.   German officers mistreating townspeople, shoving them to the ground etc.;

4.   the burgermeister not allowing Liesel to come and read with his wife, even though he had saved his own books from the fire;

5.   the teacher refusing to protect Liesel when she discovers the girl cannot read or write; and

6.   town citizens reporting each other to the authorities.

The good is seen by scenes that show:

1.   how Hans does all he can to make Liesel comfortable; he shows her love and teaches her to read;

2. Hans and Rosa taking Max into their home and hiding him, although they barely had enough to eat themselves;

3. Hans was the only one in town to speak up for a man found to have been born Jewish when the authorities come to take him away;

4. Ilsa taking Liesel under her wing and letting her be exposed to the books, knowing that her husband would disapprove;

5. Liesel sharing stories with Max to help him know what was happening in the outside world;

6. Rudy instantly being there for Liesel on the first day of school: "I thought you might need a friend," and always being there for her as the years went by; and

7. Liesel reading to calm those in the bomb shelter.

All of these scenes help the viewer take note of our humanity even in trying times.

Hopefully, you are now able to understand how themes are conveyed throughout a film and that the various pieces must be remembered and put together at its conclusion. As you progress in learning more about this topic, you will be able to make note of little details that mean nothing at the time they are seen, but link to something else much later in the film.

As Münsterberg pointed out nearly 100 years ago, memory is an essential process for the enjoyment and understanding of a film. Recall that in the Introduction of this book I stated:

> None of these processes can help us without memory. For each successive shot and scene to have meaning the viewer must be able to remember the previous shots and the prior scenes. Through the image, speech, music and other sounds the movie can suggest to our memory what it needs to recall.

CHAPTER SIXTEEN

In Conclusion

Merriam-Webster's dictionary defines *art* as "something that is created with imagination and skill and that is beautiful or that expresses important ideas or feelings." I can think of no better way to describe a film and each of the various elements contained within it. *Art appreciation* is having the knowledge, background, and understanding of the qualities that comprise any work of art. This book is a guide to identifying and understanding the qualities that comprise the artistic elements of film. There is a lot more to learn and experience, but if you take the first steps toward using them to help you see, hear, feel, and resonate with what emanates from a screen.

Use the following exercises to begin your enhanced exploration:

1. Visit your local art museum or institute and find a classic painting; look at it for a least twenty to thirty minutes. Take note of the brush strokes, the use of the paint and the colors, the details as presented by the artist. Try to let the painting speak to you and take note of your reaction. No sooner than two weeks later, go back and repeat the exercise with the same painting. What details

do you see now that you didn't earlier, and do you feel differently about the painting?

2. Obtain a DVD of a movie that also includes a special-features section, and particularly look for one with a commentary by the director or a critic. Watch the film; then watch the special features. Watch the film again in a day or two. Did you get more out of the movie the second time? An excellent training commentary is Roger Ebert's running commentary found on the *70th Anniversary Edition of Casablanca*. (Note: you will need to watch the film first, since the commentary overrides the sound.)

3. Watch a movie you have previously seen and enjoyed. Pick an element you are going to pay particular attention to. As the movie progresses, make notes about how the filmmakers address *that* element. How are their decisions affecting the movie? How does their use of that element affect your mental and visceral responses to various scenes? In any given scene, does how the element is being used enhance or distract from the movie and the story? One author suggests that by asking yourself *why* a scene was included or a cinematic device or technique used, you can begin to see the meaning expressed. [1]

---

1 Ryan and Lenos, *An Introduction to Film Analysis*, 8.

"Ask yourself why the filmmakers did something a particular way. Why is the camera where it is? Why are certain colors being used? Why does the image look as it does? Try to determine what idea the filmmakers had in mind when they constructed an image in a particular way. How does the way this image is made relate to the characters in the film? Or to the issues and conflicts that move the plot forward?" [2]

4. Watch lots of films. It has often been said that to become film savvy, one must watch the classics that demonstrate the principles of cinema. Get a list of the Academy Award nominees in each of the elemental categories from the last twenty years, and start watching them. Remember that the nominations are made by Academy members in each of the crafts, so they have credibility. See if you can detect why they were nominated. Can you identify what has changed over the years? If nothing else, you will see some great films.

5. Another great method for understanding the art of film is to become acquainted with various techniques in certain time periods: Why were they developed? How they were used, and how did later filmmakers mimic them? The best tool to accom-

---

2 Ibid., 28.

plish this is Mark Cousins' *The Story of Film: An Odyssey*, DVD set, Music Box Films, 2011.

6. In order to help you learn how to determine a movie's themes and meaning, try the following exercise: Take a notepad with you to the movie. As the movie progresses, write what is happening. After the film, go back and read your notes. As cryptic as they may be, they will describe a number of themes and your memory will help you fill in the balance.

The Appendix includes a number of enlightening interview excerpts from a myriad of filmmakers discussing their various crafts. Sometimes it's best to hear directly from them about how those working on a film saw their roles and made their decisions to present the material in a certain way.

Go to the library and check out the many books and films on the art of filmmaking. Subscribe to some of the top film magazines, such as *Film Comment*, *Sight and Sound*, and *Filmmaker*. Attend local organizations that screen new movies and then hold post-screening discussions, or join a neighborhood movie group led by an expert.

Lastly, I recommend attending at least one of the major film festivals each year. Many of the films shown at the festivals are followed by a session with the filmmakers.

The more you understand, the more you will enjoy any movie.

APPENDICES

In Their Own Words

Consistent with the view I stated in the Introduction that the filmmakers' own words and thoughts will help you become a better movie watcher, I am providing a series of excerpts from interviews of filmmakers in various roles.

John Sayles, Screenwriter and Director

Alfred Hitchcock, Director

Stephen Goldblatt, Cinematographer

David Lean, British Director and Film Editor

James Cameron, Screenwriter and Director

Walter Murch, Film Editor

Steven Spielberg, Screenwriter and Director

François Truffaut, French Screenwriter and Director

Nora Ephron, Screenwriter and Director

Meryl Streep, Actress

Anne Coates, Film Editor

John Sayles, Screenwriter and Director

The following are excerpts from an illuminating interview with John Sayles about *Lone Star* that was conducted by Tod Lippy in New York City. It is one of the best interviews of a filmmaker that I know. The full interview will help the reader see how much of what is discussed in this book is put into play in real life. It was first published in the September 1996 edition of *Scenario: The magazine of screenwriting art*. (Vol. 2, No. 2. , PP. 50-53 and 192-196). I urge the reader to find the issue and read the full interview.

JS: "[I]n *Lone Star*, the main thing I wanted to do was to make the transitions to the past seamless, either done without a cut at all-using a pan-or with dissolves.

TL: I assume that kind of thing was incorporated to signal the immediacy of the past in the lives of these characters.

JS: Yeah. I didn't want any hard transitions. Also, in several cases, the person who starts the story is not the person who finishes it. It was a way of suggesting that kind of shared past that's still in the town, even though it's not written history. The who-did-what-to-whom is still informing who does what to whom now. I wanted that feeling especially for the character of Sam. He's someone who's doing everything because of the past. He didn't want to be to be sheriff: if his father had never been sheriff he never would have wanted to be. So he acts as our voyager into the past, and what he finds is not necessarily what you want him to find, or expect him to find, but he's definitely our guide.

TL: You've talked in the past about the importance of a "guide" character in the types of films you make-someone to help the audience navigate through the story.

JS: It's important that sometimes the audience knows more than he does, so that you're not limited to what he sees. Sometimes, when he leaves, we stay. Del Payne's whole story is sort of parallel to that, which is what you often find in those towns, which can still be pretty segregated. It was interesting to me that there could be two fairly similar stories going on, but in parallel universes. And those characters never meet. At one point, I was thinking that maybe this should be like *City of Hope*, where there's at least one scene where everybody meets everybody else. But then I realized, "No, these guys don't need to meet. They only meet through intermediaries, like Otis."

* * * *

"**TL**: *Lone Star* features fifty-odd speaking parts. Did you write character biographies for each one?

JS: I write them after I finish the script, for the actors, because I never do rehearsals. What I do is send them all these one- or two-page synopses--"this is who your character is; this is your backstory, where you are emotionally right now"-so that they don't invent that shit. I don't want to be on the set and find them playing something a certain way, and when I ask why, they say, "Oh, my uncle burned me with an iron when I was 5 years old." Because actors will do that, they'll fill it in if they think they need to. So I'd rather fill it in for them, so they're grounded. So much of movie acting is about the moment. If they know where they're coming from before we even start shooting, then they really can play the moment. Especially with a low budget, where you're not going to want to do it a million times. So anyway, I don't write biographies beforehand. I usually go in knowing some sequences: this is where I want to start- this is where I want to end.

TL: Did you write each of these plots as a contiguous story, or did you combine them from the beginning?

JS: I had a bunch of scenes and just started writing. In fact, I didn't know who shot Charley Wade until I was about three-quarters of the way through. Sam and I were in the same boat. I mean, there were three suspects: Did I want it to be his father, Otis or Hollis? Hollis just made the most sense. For a while there I thought it might be Otis, but then I couldn't really imagine Buddy taking that kind of risk for a guy he didn't know that well. I would have had to invent some kind of reason why they knew each other from before.

TL: So you didn't, for instance, write the entire story of Del Payne and his family as one unit?

JS: No. I had already outlined it, and I'd just write each scene as I got to it. Occasionally I'd write a very long scene and then chop it up in several pieces. But then just as often I'd put it back together again, or just condense it. . . .."

* * * *

"**TL:** I remember reading an interview with you from some time back, where you mentioned director Allen Dwan's theorem for ascertaining whether a particular character is essential to the story or not. He felt that the character had to have at least two lines of emotional connection to the other charac-ters in order to serve a purpose.

JS: Uh-huh. I call it "glue.".....

* * * *

"**TL**: This is your first "mystery" film, although it's certainly much more than a simple whodunit. It has certain similarities, especially if you think about its second and final revelation, to a film like *Chinatown*. Was that film in your mind at all when you were writing this?

JS: You know, I looked at *Chinatown* more for wide-screen than for anything else. . . . .. Mostly what I thought about was that I wanted a double ending-two climaxes. They give Sam two choices to make. First, what he's gonna do with history, because he's put in the position where he gets to write it after learning the truth about Charley Wade's death. So he makes this choice to let the legend take care of it, including letting the legend take a little heat, which doesn't fuck his father up the way he almost wanted to. The second choice is what, personally, he is going to do about society."

* * * *

"**TL**: Do you feel that your experience as an actor has helped you to write better parts for actors?

JS: Oh, absolutely. .... And what I try to do with my
characters is figure out what each particular
person's point of view is about each event. . . .

So basically, in every scene, you go from that.
You put two people together with different points
of view. It's what I do as a director. I go over in
the corner with one actor and talk to them about
what they should be thinking about in a particular scene, and then do the same with the other
actor. And then you adjust it to get the right
emotional tone. You want to set up an interesting dynamic, and that's what I try to do in the
writing as well. Another thing I was thinking about
was having Sam always ask very direct questions,
and then having everybody respond to him in
metaphors-.-that's something I really wanted to
have throughout. . . .

"So in fact it's not only about how they see the
world; it's about their rhythm of talking. That's
another thing you get from acting; it's another way
to separate one character from another. Do they
use metaphors, or are they very direct?"

* * * *

"TL: You often open a scene with a close-up of an
object, such as the fishing lure in the scene at the
lake with Hollis and Sam. Is this purely practical?

JS: Most always, if it's meant to be a time cut, you just want something to refocus things. What a cut should do is refocus, or even confuse the audience, make them say, "Where am I?" That "Where am I?" takes the place of "Three months later ..." Sometimes you want a kind of association with that object, like in thrillers, where you see the knife before the murder happens. But also, sometimes you do it in a scene because the next one takes place in the same spot, which I hate to do too often. You know, they're cleaning the kitchen in the first scene, and in the next, the eggs are sizzling in the frying pan, and then you say, "Okay, it must be the next morning at breakfast...."

"In *Lone Star*, for instance, instead of cutting to the face of a sergeant who's out of uniform, who you may not recognize, you cut to these weird piles of bullets and weird sculptures, and you hope people will think, "That guy we met earlier made art out of bullets or something," and they'll know where they are. Instead of losing the first few lines of conversation, having to waste the first three or four lines before people settle into a scene."

****

"TL: What about the scene which occurs near the beginning of the movie, in which the parents and

teachers meet to discuss changes in curriculum in
the public school?

JS: That was always there, and I always wanted Pilar to
be there, in the center of it. It's not something that
she necessarily thinks about later on in the film,
but once again, it shows those parallel universes:
history as a family thing, and as a social phenom-
enon. Is there a "we" here, or is it just "your story"
and "my story"? If my kids are going to go to
public school and I pay taxes, do we have to hear
the minority group's version of history?

What this basically involved was a geographical decision: I decided to make the meeting
smaller, and in the form of a circle, so things are
coming from every side, as opposed to a prosce-
nium situation, where somebody comes up to the
microphone and faces this tribunal of the people
in power. Here, there's some question about who's
in power: teachers or parents? That's the struggle
that goes on in public schools all over the place
now. It's a very sensitive issue."

Alfred Hitchcock, Director

The following are excerpted from Hitchcock's essay *Direction.*[1]

"...films suffer from their own power of appealing to millions. They could often be subtler than they are, but their own popularity won't let them."

* * * *

"So you gradually build up the psychological situation, piece by piece, using the camera to emphasize first one detail, then another. The point is to draw the audience right inside the situation instead of leaving them to watch it from the outside, from a distance. And you can do this only by breaking the action up into details and cutting from one to the other, so that each detail is forced in turn on the attention of the audience and reveals its psychological meaning. If you played the whole scene straight through, and simply made a photographic record of it with the camera always in one position, you would lose your power over the audience. They would watch the scene without becoming really involved in it, and you would have no means of concentrating their attention on those particular visual details which make them feel what the characters are feeling.

* * * *

1 Alfred Hitchcock, Charles Davy, ed., *Footnotes to the Film* (London, England: Lovat Dickson and Thompson, Ltd., 1937).

"This way of building up a picture means that film work hasn't much need for the virtuoso actor who gets his effects and climaxes himself, who plays directly on to the audience with the force of his talent and personality. The screen actor has got to be much more plastic, he has to submit himself to be used by the director and the camera."....."I must say that in recent years I have come to make much less use of obvious camera devices. I have become more commercial minded, afraid that anything at all subtle may be missed. I have learnt from experience how easily small touches are overlooked." [2]

2 Author's note: Mr. Hitchcock's comment on subtlety is one of the distinctions referred to in Chapter 5 of this book: *Significant Differences in European and American Films.*

Stephen Goldblatt, Cinematographer

Steven Goldblatt worked with director Alan Pakula on *The Pelican Brief* (1993). The movie was shot in sequence, a rarity in American filmmaking. The following is Goldblatt discussing his art, excerpted from *Contemporary Cinematographers and Their Art*:

"As much as possible, this [shooting in sequence] allowed us to make sure the character transitions were real and the story development would ring true.

Just as a well-crafted story keeps the audience's attention, well-crafted visual moves hold their attention as well. Each of the transitions in this picture was carefully planned. The film grammar supports the story and holds the audience's interest.

If we had a wide shot for one exposition, we could cut to a tighter shot for the next. If one was surreal, the next would be angry or exciting. A writer's job is to guide the emotions with words, a cinematographer's job is to do the same thing with visuals."

Goldblatt added: 'There is more to making a movie than lights, cameras and lenses," he says "There is also composition. ... Writers take audiences through emotional steps, so do cinematographers. We plan the transitions with the director. If one scene is wide, we try to make the next tight. If one is high and sweeping, even surreal, we try to make the next angry and exciting. Take a look at the opening - it was sweeping vistas of endangered marshes. The dissolve? To the crowd outside the Supreme Court.

Each transition does a specific job. We don't have to go from close up to close up. Unless of course, it is right for the story." [1]

1 Pauline Rogers, *Contemporary Cinematographers and Their Art* (Oxford, England: Butterworth-Heinemann, 1998), 85.

David Lean, British Director and Editor

Lean is best known for a number of epic films, such as *Bridge on the River Kwai, Lawrence of Arabia, Doctor Zhivago*, and *A Passage to India*. The following excerpted interviews were originally conducted by Kevin Brownlow and are now found in the book *David Lean Interviews*. [1]

KB: That brings up the issue of directing actors. How was it that you had absolutely no experience in stage work, yet you were able to cope with actors?

DL: It was terrifying. You see that's another thing about the cutting room. In the cutting room you are correcting, a lot of the time, mistakes in performances. You'll take a line, the sound track from take five and put it on the picture of take one. All sorts of fancy fakery like that. You'll cut to someone else's face when he or she gives a wrong intonation. Suppose later, I more or less copied him. On *In Which We Serve* I had a very nice cast, you know, very nice people, and I just found myself obeying my instincts and with a great heave of moral courage said what I thought to them. And most of the time they listened to me. Anyhow, I gradually learnt.

1 Steven Organ, ed., *David Lean Interviews* (Jackson: University Press of Mississippi, 2009).

In discussing his problems working with Rex Harrison, Lean relates that "You have to have a lot of courage to say, "No, it's exactly the same. Cut. Let's go again." And this happened and in the end we were looking at each other across the set with completely blank faces. Not one of us giving way. So I said, "Rex, I know you think I have no experience and am no good as a director, but I think I'm a bloody good cutter, and if you don't say and do what I say in this particular instance, I'll leave you in shreds on the floor." He did it the way I wanted.

> **DL:** ... you see film acting is in fact thinking. If some-
> body is running away from having murdered
> somebody, running down the street, and you have
> that small figure running away from the camera,
> if they're thinking correctly, they will run and
> walk correctly, because the thought dictates the
> walk. So I take a lot of trouble explaining to actors
> the atmosphere I'm trying to get. Then I talk to
> them about the situation they are in and gradually,
> hopefully, suggest to them what they're thinking.
> Most of the time that works. I'm often amazed by
> the way actors come up to me at the end of the
> day and say, "I cannot thank you enough. You were
> so helpful. I've never had this before." And all I've
> done, it always turns out, is given them a little
> confidence and a kind of tour of the scene we were
> doing, and it helped them over the humps.

KB: If I looked at one of your cutting copies, would there just be one splice or multiple?

DL: You would find the cutting copy absolutely filled with buildup and patches where I've changed my mind. I'll tell you another thing that I didn't mention to you. Half the thing of cutting- it's like acting. It's a question of balance. If you make a long shot run for eight feet, it's heavier than a long shot running for six feet. I call that absolute balance and very often if you alter the length of the long shot you probably have to add something to the close-up. But it's cutting from or cutting to that creates this balance.

Now editing is, as I say, telling a story in pictures. I also have to decide what the audience sees and when. You may think this rather curious: up to now I've always waited until a film is finished before I attempt to cut it. I start at the first scene and I go on from there because if I do that I get the excitement of telling a story from the first sentence on the first page. So I think, "We never start with a long shot. Wait a minute, what would happen if I started with a close-up and disclosed the long shot a bit later? Let them into the situation by degrees." I go through this process shot-by-shot.

It's the putting together of an enormous jigsaw puzzle. And the audience should feel that there are not any cuts. I mean, a cut from you to a close-up

of me, or a close-up of me and a door, that's a cut
you should be unaware of. If somebody goes out
and slams the door and you have two pictures of
the door slamming then cut to the person watching, and the echo of the door slamming is over
that close-up, you'll never know you made a cut.
It's got to be as smooth as knife going through
butter.. . .

James Cameron, Screenwriter and Director

The following excerpts from an interview by Tavis Smiley are about *Avatar* and took place on December 17, 2009. It is recounted in *James Cameron: Interviews*. [1]

TS: You mentioned earlier a number of themes that run through the film. We'll talk about the environmental theme in just a second, because I assume that was deliberate, given that you were behind the project. What also is fascinating for me about the project is to your earlier point here, in this *Avatar* film, the humans are invading. To my mind, at least, there's some interesting-I'm trying to find the right word here - some interesting commentary that you allow us, force us to wrestle with about who we are as humans, how we treat the planet, how we treat other beings.

JC: Our fellow humans.

TS: Exactly. Tell me more about that.

JC: Well, yeah, I think that was deliberate and it was one of the themes that I wanted to explore in this, and there are obviously references to Vietnam,

1 Brent Dunham, ed., James Cameron: Interviews *(Conversations with Filmmakers Series)* (Jackson: University Press of Mississippi, 2012), 191–193.

there are references to Iraq, there are references
to the American colonial period, and we've got
a history-and not just America, obviously; we're
talking about the French, the Spanish, the English,
the Portuguese-of just kind of invading and taking
what we need and forcing out and marginalizing
indigenous cultures, and sometimes wiping them
out completely, to the point that we don't have
that many truly indigenous cultures left in this
world. They're very, very tiny and there's a few in
the Amazon, a few in Papua New Guinea. Some
of these languages are going extinct almost on a
daily basis, some of these dialects. So we have a
terrible history with this, and I sort of extrapolated
even farther, to this idea of entitlement. We do the
same thing with nature-we take what we need and
we don't give back, and we've got to start giving
back. We've got to start seriously and aggressively
accepting our responsibility for stewardship of
this planet.

TS: How do you give—my word, not yours—the
proper treatment to the issues that you've just laid
out now that we're all going to be forced to wrestle
with when we see the film? As a filmmaker, I
assume, at least, you want us to marinate on some
of these things beyond the theater experience.
How do you do that without being preachy?

JC: Yeah, it's a fine line. First of all you've got to put
    a whole bunch of spoonfuls of sugar in there
    to make it an adventure, make it visual, make it
    exciting. People are telling me coming out of the
    theater that they cried three times and they're
    having this big kind of emotional reaction, so
    that's part of it. The other thing is just don't make
    it preachy. Don't assume you have to give people
    information. Assume that they've got the informa-
    tion already, and what we're going to give you is an
    emotional reaction to how we relate to nature and
    take you on a journey, not just a physical journey
    through the world but a kind of a mental journey,
    where you wind up looking at things from the side
    of the Na'vi, with their deep respect for nature,
    and then looking back at ourselves from that.

TL: That's what science fiction does so well-it can hold
    up a mirror to all of us without pushing specific
    buttons of you're worse than-this guy's worse than
    this guy, you see what I mean? Science fiction
    doesn't really predict the future, that's not what
    it's there for. It's there to hold a mirror up to the
    present and look at the human condition, some-
    times from the outside.

Walter Murch, Film Editor

Author Michael Ondaatje interviewed the legendary editor for his book *The Conversations: Walter Murch and the Art of Editing Film* published by Alfred A Knopf in 2002. The following are some excerpts in which he discusses his craft.

* * * * *

MO: It's an odd thing: I've heard you talk before about the importance of ambiguity in film, and the need to save that ambiguous quality which exists in a book or painting, and which you think a film does not often have. And at the same time in a mix you are trying to "perfect" that ambiguity.

WM: I know. It's a paradox. And one of the most fruit-ful paradoxes, I think, is that even when the film is finished, there should be unsolved problems. Because there's another stage, beyond the finished film: when the audience views it. You want the audience to be co-conspirators in the creation of this work, just as much as the editor or the mixers or the cameraman or the actors are. If by some chemistry you actually did remove all ambiguity in the final mix-even though it had been ambig-uous up to that point-I think you would do the film a disservice. But the paradox is that you have to approach every problem as if it's desperately

important to solve it. You can't say, I don't want to
solve this because it's got to be ambiguous. If you
do that, then there's a sort of hemorrhaging of
the organism.

* * * * *

MO: Are there other scenes you remember editing a
certain way which were then scrapped and eventually recut in another way?

WM: The closest would be the final confession
between Almásy and Caraveggio in *The English
Patient*. Very late in the editing we altered it from a
private dialogue between two people to one where
a third person, Hana, overhears the Patient's
confession. She was not a part of that scene when
it was shot. But inserting her presence into the
conversation allowed her to have the important
knowledge about who Almásy was-which Caravag-
gio alone had had in the screenplay and during the
shooting-so that when she later administers the
fatal dose of morphine to Almásy she does it with
the weight of that knowledge. So we used footage
of her from a scene we had dropped, where she
was with Kip-and in one case we actually removed
Kip from the frame, optically, to give Hana a
whole frame to herself.

MO: What was remarkable was how her emotion from that earlier scene with Kip was immediately altered, and now expressed something new in this different context. Also, that artificial link brought the various narrative threads in the film together. It's a wonderful example of lateral thinking during the editing process-this can be in a book or a film-that to me is as creative as the original composition. It's the art of shaking a scene up, turning it upside down, to discover other possibilities in the written or filmed work.

I also remember, in an early cut of *The English Patient*, a scene after Hana says good-bye to Kip, who is on his motorbike, where she walks back to the house. There was an amazing shot of her back-her whole body expressing great loss. A great shot. But in the next cut of the film it was gone. Her grief there, over Kip's leaving, was too dose to the grief of the *Patient's* last scene. You couldn't leave it in, because you had to pace the film. You needed, I suppose, to save the grief for the next scene. You had to remove what was a remarkable shot for the value of the film as a whole.

WM: Yes, that's what I call the "Tragedy-of-Job moments." They are like the good man Job, who does everything-and more-that God requests of him, but God perversely afflicts him and not the bad person who is Job's neighbour. Why me? Job asks. Well, it's because God can see the whole that

Job cannot see, and in some mysterious way these afflictions are for the good of the whole, in a way that is invisible to the person.

There was a moment in *The Conversation*-it had to do with Harry Caul's initial assembly of his tape recording of the lovers-that was in every cut of the film, and somehow any changes in nearby scenes had to be reflected in it. It was like a hinge scene. Over and over again I would be working on that scene, and it would accept the changes, it would accommodate itself to the whole. If you anthropomorphized, you could see the scene becoming prouder and prouder of itself, of how it did all this for the film! And yet there came a point when I said, You know, I think I'm going to remove this scene. Everything else is now so clear that this scene no longer needs to be in there. It's making the point that is made elsewhere in the film.

Stephen Spielberg, Screenwriter and Director

The following Spielberg comments are from various sources. In the first segment, he discusses *Empire of the Sun* (1987). [1]

"For the first time, I am making a movie to satisfy me, not the audience."

"One of the things I responded to in the book," Spielberg says, "was the fact that it made selections of what a child grabs on to with his eyes compared to what an adult would see. Kids in their imaginations just create these amazing real-time scenarios that are triggered by what they choose to look at. The book was filled with visual references. And that's what I really responded to, being able to tell this story through the eyes of a child, and to show the child losing all that. It's about the death of childhood. The story is probably quintessentially more about the death of childhood than anything I've made before or since.

"I wanted to draw a parallel story between the death of this boy's innocence and the death of the innocence of the entire world. When that white light goes off in Nagasaki and the boy witnesses the light – whether he really sees it or his mind sees it doesn't matter. Two innocents have come to an end and a heartbroken world has begun."

---

1 Richard Schickel, *Steven Spielberg: A Retrospective* (New York: Sterling Publishing, 2012), 116.

* * * * *

The following excerpt is Spielberg on working with cameramen (as moderated by James Powers, May 1978).

"The best situation I find is when cameramen like the same movies I like, or the same artwork. Vilmos [Zsigmond] and I looked at a lot of Norman Rockwell together before *Sugarland Express* (1974). I like a cameraman who is open-minded and will try absolutely anything, and who can work fast, meaning I don't like to sit around when the actors are prepared and fired up to do a scene waiting while the cameraman lights a room this size. There are cameramen who would spend six hours lighting this room! Vilmos and Bill Butler, who shot *Jaws* (1975), are both fast and very good.

Vilmos and I had a very good relationship. He has one of the best eyes in town. We would share ideas: "Wouldn't it be better to shoot this scene in a master from forty feet back rather than break it up and cover it?" Sometimes I would agree, sometimes not, and every time I said "I prefer my idea to your idea," he would step down and do it my way. There was never any dissonance. I worked with Bill a little differently because we're old friends. I found myself being more autocratic, not because I trusted Bill any less that I trusted Vilmos, but because *Jaws* was such a personal responsibility that I had to call every shot. . ..To cut off the relationship between myself and the viewfinder would be like denying my existence to the film world." [2]

---

2 George Stevens Jr., *Conversations at the American Film Institute with the Great Moviemakers, The Next Generation* (New York: Vintage Books, 2012), 615.

All of the following excerpted interviews are taken from conversations that occurred as part of the ongoing series of seminars at the American Film Institute in Hollywood, California.

* * * * *

François Truffaut, French Screenwriter and Director

The following interview was moderated by James Powers, February 1979.

JP: Do you have a particular technique when it comes to screenwriting?

FT: In order to feel good about making a film, I have to believe that the general concept is a strong one. When I was a journalist years ago, I noticed everyone usually reworked the first things they wrote, and then rushed the rest, which was inevitably flawed. I decided always to do the contrary. I begin a film only if I'm positive that the last fifteen minutes are going to be good. Even when I start the editing, I begin by working on the last two reels. After all, it's towards the end of a film that an audience is more demanding. I often have very laborious exposition in my films and recently have been trying to begin a film right in the

middle of the action to avoid the exposition, but it
remains difficult.

On the other hand, the audience is very nice
about the first twenty minutes of a film. They
accept that it's going to take a little bit of time for
the story to get under way, but by the fifth reel
these things have to come together. Many of the
scripts of my films are ideas that I've been thinking
about for a few years. Those which remain longest
in my head are those that are most difficult to
make, like *Adele H.* or *The Green Room*. These things
stay in my head for six or seven years before I
even decide to make the film. But those years are
never lost, because once a year I'll get a sudden
great idea about one of the stories." [1]

JP: Do you think storytelling in cinema has changed
over the years?

FT: What I've been thinking about these last few years,
besides color, is that the variety of visual elements
that used to be enriching to a film no longer are.
You remember that in films twenty years ago there
were love scenes, chase scenes, scenes out in the
country. They tried to give the audience a variety
of elements. They thought variety was a positive
thing, and I thought so, too. I'm talking about
the time when people went to the same movie

1 Ibid., 694–695.

house every week, no matter what was playing. But I think since television has assumed such an important role in our lives, variety is no longer a value to be desired. Very simply, if you watch the news for a half an hour, within that news broadcast you already have all the forms of cinema that exist. You have interviews, reportage, you have candid camera, you have a clip from a film that has opened in town, you have a few commercials that cost a fortune to make and are perfectly executed. So it seems to me, by contrast, when you go into a movie theater, you want to see something more rigorous.

It's in this spirit that I made films like *Adele H.* Fifteen years ago, in a film like that, I would have shown all kinds of detail of the period itself, but I enclosed the film around Isabelle Adjani. It was a close-up of her, an attempt to construct emotion through unity. In the past, variety was a kind of insurance against boredom. If people don't like this part, at least they'll like the following scene. I don't know if you agree with me, but if you see films from thirty or forty years ago, the films that remain most solid are the ones that give the impression of being closed. In other words, they are films in which there are no natural elements. There is something claustrophobic about them. There are certain films in which if a bicycle passes by when you are shooting, that bicycle remains in the film. But you don't have bicycles in the films of Dreyer or Eisenstein, and not in Hitchcock's films, either. I think a film that remains as fantastic thirty years later is *The Big Sleep* by Howard Hawks. Or *Rear Window*, in which there wasn't a single natural thing in the film. Or *Sunrise* by Murnau. It seems to me that the films that hold up best are artificial ones, rather than the ones that try to stay close to life." [2]

---

2 Ibid., 681–691.

Nora Ephron, Screenwriter and Director

Nora Ephron was originally hired to do a script rewrite for the movie *Sleepless in Seattle* (1993). When the director didn't like what was done to the script and refused to proceed, Ephron was then hired to direct it. Her cinematographer was Sven Nykvist, the world-renowned cameraman for almost all of Ingmar Bergman's movies.

The following excerpted interview was moderated by Lynn Roth, September 1993.

LR: How did you become involved in *Sleepless in Seattle*?

NE: I was the fourth writer. It already had a director. Kim Basinger was kind of interested in doing it, if you can believe it, and they wanted a three-week rewrite and sent it to me. I had done *This Is My Life* for Directors Guild scale and it wasn't enough to keep me going for a year, so I was looking for a fast killing and I took on this rewrite....

Then they sent me *Sleepless in Seattle*. I looked at it and it was a very gloopy script. It was nothing like the movie that you saw-nothing like it. It was not a comedy at all. There were about two little jokes in it-the kid had the jokes. One of them was "Jed's got cable," which gets a laugh, you know. I hadn't read the original Jeff Arch screenplay,

which I eventually read after we finished shooting,
which is interesting if anyone wants to look at the
progress of the story, just for fun. In the original
version the father made the phone call to the
radio shrink. He not only made one phone call, he
made six phone calls, and they went like this: I'm
so sad and droopy. My wife died and I don't know
what to do." Clunk! It was an unmakeable movie
because no male actor would ever have played a
wuss like this. Ever. By the time I got to the movie,
David Ward, who's a very good screenwriter, had
done a couple of rewrites and made the fundamental change that made it all possible-he had the
kid make the phone call....

Sometimes the studio will say to you that it just
needs "character" when the truth is that all it is is
a character piece, so the main thing it's missing
is the thing that it is. Neither of the characters
existed in any way. They weren't likable people,
but there was this sort of fabulous dirt that you
could grow wonderful grass in if you just knew
how to do it. There was the idea of destiny, the
idea of the global village-which wasn't remote-
ly fleshed in. You could see that you could have
enormous fun doing things called "Everybody in
America tells the same jokes, reads the same books,
has the same statistics, knows that it's easier to be
killed by a terrorist than to find a husband after
the age forty.

The idea of the little boy who wants his father
to find a wife and who wants a new mother was all
there. They just hadn't been done. The idea of *An
Affair to Remember* was in there, it just wasn't funny.
And even though the screenplay wasn't particularly
good, the last scene, on the Empire State Building,
was great. It was powerful. So I thought, "I know
how to make these people into people and how
to give the thing some drive." I did a three-week
rewrite and put in my favorite character-Jessi-
ca, who's the most autobiographical character in
it-just a completely hopeless, bossy human being.

I turned this screenplay in and what happened
then was really kind of funny, because I'd never
been through it in my life and I never will again. It
was like a teeny-weeny explosion. In forty-eight
hours, every agent, every actor in Hollywood
wanted to be in this movie-except for Kim Basinger. And the original director didn't want anything
to do with it, because I think he knew it had
become a comedy and I don't think he thought
it should be a comedy. So off he went, and when
the dust settled they offered it to me to direct. I
said, "You know, this is not ready to go. This needs
a huge amount more work. This doesn't begin to
have the kind of texture that I like in a movie.

I have this fanatical thing about having every
single character in a movie have a moment. Even
the guy who delivers the mail has a little scene.
He doesn't just give the mail, he's got this dopey

conversation about hiccup cures. I want every actor who comes into a movie to have a reason for being there. I want to get good actors to come because they'll know that even if they only have one scene, it'll be a good scene. If they say to someone, "I was Meg Ryan's brother," they'll say, "Oh yes, I remember that scene."

I want that, not just because I want good actors, but because it makes a thin movie. This is a thin, character-driven movie, and because you don't have suspense, you don't have car crashes, you don't have guns, all you want is delicious character things. You know the scene where Rita Wilson tells the story about *An Affair to Remember* and starts to cry? There's no reason for it. It doesn't move the plot along. But you just can't imagine the movie without it, because that's what the movie is. All the little themes of this movie come together in that scene-about women and men and how different they are. [1]

LR: We should probably mention Sven Nykvist.

NE: Yes, we should mention Sven. One of the reasons why my second movie is better than my first, besides that I had $25 million to spend compared to $9 million, is that I was able to hire the world's greatest cinematographer. It was my second movie

---

1 Ibid., 161–162.

and I think it was his one hundred and second.
Very few cinematographers can do what Sven can
do. He loves working with long scenes, because all
Ingmar Bergman did was long scenes. They would
shoot ten-minute scenes and then cut because the
film ran out. Sven always says, "Faces and teacups"-
his career has been faces and teacups.

He's not like Michael Ballhaus, who's a great
cinematographer but is always wanting to move
the camera around the table, whether it matters
or not. I'm never going to have a camera moving
around a table in a movie because what is this
about? It's just about the camera moving around
the table. And Sven can light in two seconds,
because he didn't have any lights when he was
working with Bergman. Fanny and Alexander was
shot with candles.

And that scene where Tom Hanks goes out on
a date, when he goes over and says, "The ipecac is
in the cabinet, in case either of you drinks poison,"
you can't see Tom because he's in the part of the
kitchen where there is no light. I cannot tell you
how many cinematographers would have wasted
ninety minutes putting a key light there so Tom
would not be in the dark. Sven doesn't care about
that. Some people are in the dark and some
people are in the light. Everything is so gorgeous.
Meg's skin – he's fantastic about skin and he's
always screaming at the makeup people about not

having much makeup so that people will look as if they are alive. Sven is the greatest person." [2]

---

2 Ibid., 163.

Meryl Streep, Actress

The following excerpted interview was moderated by Jon
Avnet, May 2004.

JA: Can you talk about the character of Joanna Kramer?

MS: There is a little bit of teeny pattern in characters
that I'm drawn to —not necessarily everything that
I've done. I like to defend characters that would
otherwise be misconstrued or misunderstood.
Joanna Kramer was one of the earliest ones, but
certainly it goes further back. I remember when
I grew up in my hometown, we knew the two
people that had been divorced-it was very unusual
that people would divorce. But then the sixties
happened, the seventies, and then custody battles
started being very intense. I didn't understand
Joanna in the book. Her motivation wasn't clear
to me.

Robert Benton, who is a great soul and a
compassionate human being, felt the same way.
He was looking for a way not to explain Joanna, but
understand her. I like the idea of being a translator
of a person to people who wouldn't maybe cross
the street to meet her. When *Kramer vs. Kramer*
came out it was new, but now it seems like everybody comes from two families. Usually the courts

awarded the mother custody, and then there was this huge backlash against that. *Kramer vs. Kramer* played into that rage. Most of the movie was about Dustin's relationship with his son, whom he had ignored for most of the first five years of his life.

I didn't know Dustin before we started working. On the first day working together, he slapped me as hard as he could across my face-it sort of set up the stakes. I remember going, "Is this supposed to be acting?" It was intense but I just reacted and that was easy. The second part was the courtroom stuff after Joanna has disappeared for most of the movie and then comes back and makes a plea to be reinvolved in her son's life. There was some question about the courtroom testimony-what to say-and everybody had their different ideas. Benton said, "Everybody write in a paragraph what you think she would say." Dustin was thrilled because he had very strong opinions about what she should say, and so did Benton and so did I. So we went into our little dressing rooms and wrote, and then we voted and I won. So I got to say what I wrote. It was a kind of unreal introduction to that kind of big Hollywood movie because they don't let you do that normally, but that was Benton's generosity and imagination. [1]

---

1 Ibid., 642.

What follows is Streep comparing the ending of *Bridges of Madison County* to *Kramer vs. Kramer* at An Evening of Conversation with Meryl Streep and Jane Pauley, which was conducted at Indiana University on November 12, 2010.

"Yes, the whole film [*Bridges of Madison County*] moves to that moment. It's good screenwriting when the paths have been well prepared towards this crossroad–literally a crossroad–a blinking light in the rain. The romance is all washed away, there's nothing but the choice, and the sadness of it and the finality of it.

I heard somebody say something on television the other day: 'Give them emotion, give them action, but make them wait for it.' Make the audience wait. And that's sort of the same as in *Kramer vs. Kramer* –there's a certain tension that you maintain all through that you've got to hold off till the end."

Anne Coates, Film Editor

The following excerpted interview was moderated by Philip Linson, March 2000.

PL: Are there any kinds of rules you can give us about when a cut needs to be made?

AC: Generally I don't think there are any rules when it comes to cutting. That said, I was always taught that with a well-shot scene and good acting, don't cut in until you really feel the need to see a close-up. One of the things I've done on more than one occasion when I've been brought in late, to try and save a film, is take out some of the cuts and simplify everything. I'm a great believer in letting shots breathe. Sometimes you can find the essence of the performances-and even the story-when you slow the whole thing down.

The people who hire me for jobs like that often think I'm going to make things faster, but sometimes you can slow things down and still make the film shorter. The more engaged the audience is with the characters, the quicker the story moves. The old-timers would give the editor wonderfully well-blocked master shots, but that doesn't happen very often these days. I think a master shot is also terribly important for the actors because they play

the whole scene and can interact with each other.
Running the entire scene in one go means the
actors can really feel the emotions at play. Often
performances in master shots are very different to
those in close-ups. Many actors will tell you they
save their best work for the close-ups. Actors are a
canny bunch, hoping that you'll use the close shots
rather than the master." [1]

PL: [regarding *Lawrence of Arabia* (1962)] Can you talk
about the scene where Omar Sharif comes riding
in? Whose decision was it to hold that shot for
so long?

AC: I'm sure it was David Lean's idea. I actually had
most of the picture cut together before David
finished shooting, and there were certain scenes
which needed a lot of work and some that didn't.
When it came to the mirage sequence with
Lawrence and Ali, I had thousands of feet of film
to work with. David had shot it with three cameras
about three or four times with him coming closer
and closer from a distance.

I think the most interesting thing was what John
Box, the production designer, did. He put little
black marks out in the desert so that your eye
goes to them. You're not really conscious of it, but
if you ever see the film again on a big screen you

1 Ibid., 114.

can't see them on a little television screen-you'll see that there are these stones lying there, subtly leading your eye to a certain point on the screen. We cut the scene many different ways. I was pretty young when I did that and was rather inclined to cut things off too quick. David said, "No, get the rhythm. Let it flow." [2]

PL: Can you talk about the seduction scene in Soderbergh's *Out of Sight* (1998)? Where did you get the idea to cross-cut those two scenes?

AC: In the script it was basically the bar scene followed by the bedroom scene. Originally, it was a much simpler structure. I cut the bar as one scene and it played very well, and then I cut the bedroom as a silent sequence. Then we started experimenting and getting a little more adventurous, and we start cutting the two scenes together and trying things. The idea was to mold them together, because what they were doing and what they were talking about were sort of in opposition to each other. Cutting them together made it just more sexual. We evolved the scene very slowly, matching things together, like his hand on the glass which cuts to his hand on her knee. Things like that just sort of floated together, but we didn't have any great ideas when we started. [3]

2 Ibid., 117
3 Ibid., 118.

Film Crew Roles

Below is a list of the major members of a film crew and their duties. There are many more people not listed who contribute to the final product and its success.

Art Director

Person who is in charge of and oversees the artists and craftspeople who build the movie sets.

Assistant Director

The Assistant Director is responsible for tracking the progress of the film versus the production schedule. Also responsible for preparing call sheets.

Associate Producer

Associate Producer is an individual who share the responsibility for creative and business dealings with the Executive Producer.

Background Artist

Background Artists design and/or construct the art used at the rear of a set.

Best Boy

Best Boy refers to the second-in-charge of any group, most commonly the chief assistant to the Gaffer. Females are also known as "Best Boys."

Body Double

Body Doubles are used to take the place of the actor/actress for a specific scene. Normally the Director will choose to use a Body

Double when an actor's actual body part isn't quite what is desired for a scene, or the actor declines to be nude.

Boom Operator

Boom Operators are members of the sound crew who operate the boom microphone. The boom microphone is a microphone attached to the end of a long pole. The Boom Operator extends the boom microphone over the actors, out of sight of the camera.

Camera Loader

The Camera Loader operates the clapboard, signaling the beginning of a shot. Also responsible for the actual loading of the film stock into film magazines.

Casting Director

The Casting Director auditions and helps choose all the speaking role actors in movies, television shows, and plays. Must have a wide knowledge of actors, and be able to match the talent with the role. Also serves as the liaison between Directors, actors, and their agents. Responsible for negotiating deals with agents and for obtaining contracts for each hired actor.

Choreographer

Person responsible for planning and directing all dance sequences within a movie.

Cinematographer

A Cinematographer is a person who has expertise in the art of capturing images on film or digitally. Is in charge of camera and lighting crews. Responsible for the selection and arrangement of lighting. The Director of Photography is the movie's chief Cinematographer.

Composer

Composers are musicians whose music appears in a movie's score. Most films have at least one original song written expressly for the score.

Conductor

The person who directs the orchestra's performance of the film's score.

Construction Coordinator

This person is in charge of all financial responsibilities having to do with construction including tracking, budgeting, and reporting. Also responsible for the physical integrity of the buildings created by the construction crew.

Costume Designer

Person who is directly responsible for designing the costumes in a film.

Dialog Coach

The Dialog Coach is responsible for helping an actor's speech pattern fit their character, usually by assisting with pronunciations and accents.

Director

Directors are responsible for the casting, editing, shot selection, shot composition, and script editing of a film. They are the creative source behind a movie, and must communicate to actors on the way a particular shot is to be played.

Directors usually have artistic control over all aspects of a film.

Director of Photography   See Cinematographer.

Dolly Grip   Grip specifically responsible for positioning the dolly. The dolly is a small truck that rolls along tracks and carries the camera, camera person, and occasionally the Director.

Editor   A person who performs the visual editing of a film, and is in charge of reconstructing the sequence of events within a film.

Executive Producer   Executive Producers are responsible for the overall production of a film, but are not directly involved in any of the technical aspects. Normally an Executive Producer will handle the business and legal issues relating to filmmaking.

Extra   Extras are people who do not have a speaking role and are usually used for filler in a crowd scene, or as background action. No acting experience is necessary to be an Extra.

Foley Artist   A Foley Artist 'recreates' sound effects for film, television and radio productions on a Foley Stage in a Post Production Studio.

Gaffer   The Gaffer is in charge of the electrical department.

Grip

Grips are responsible for the maintenance and positioning of equipment on a set.

Key Grip

The Key Grip is in charge of a group of Grips. Key Grips may also be the construction coordinator. Key Grips and Gaffers work closely together.

Line Producer

Responsible for day to day management of every person and operation associated with a film.

Location Manager

Location Managers are responsible for finding locations, and making arrangements with authorities for permits. Also supervises logistics associated with location.

Make-Up Artist

Supervises make-up department and applies make-up on actors.

Producer

Producers are in charge of a movie's production in all matters, except for the creative efforts of the Director. The Producer is also responsible for raising funds, hiring key personnel, and arranging for distribution.

Production Assistant

Production Assistants do various odd jobs on movie sets, including stopping traffic, acting as couriers, and fetching items from craft services. PA's are often attached directly to a specific actor or filmmaker.

Production Manager   Responsible for ordering
                                equipment, securing cast and
                                crew accommodations, and
                                other practical matters on the
                                set. Reports directly to the film's
                                Producer.

Production Sound Mixer   Mixes the different kinds of
                                sound produced to get the right
                                combination of vocalization, sound
                                effects and ambient sounds.

Property Master   The Property Master is responsible
                                for purchasing/acquiring all the
                                props used during production.

Screenwriter   The person that writes the script
                                either as an original piece or an
                                adaptation from another media.

Script Supervisor   Maintains record of what is in each
                                shot to make sure continuity is
                                maintained from shot to shot

Set Decorator   Set Decorators are in charge
                                of decorating movie sets with
                                furnishings, plants, drapery, and
                                anything filmed on an indoor or
                                outdoor set.

Set Designer   Set Designers translate a
                                Production Designer's vision
                                and ideas of the movie into a set
                                which is then used for filming. Set
                                Designers report to the Art Director

Sound Designer   Sound Designers are responsible
                                for creating and designing the
                                audio portion of a movie.

Special Effects   Creates digital shots when not
                                    possible to get live.

Supervising Sound Editor   Responsible for the final
                                    soundtrack. Supervises the sound
                                    mixer, dialogue editor, sound
                                    effects editor, music editor and
                                    assistants.

Technical Advisor   Technical Advisors are experts on
                                    a specific subject matter, and offer
                                    advice on making a film more
                                    authentic and true to its subject
                                    matter.

Unit Production Manager   Unit Production Managers are
                                    executives who are responsible for
                                    the administration of a film. They
                                    report to a senior Producer

Wrangler   Wranglers are directly responsible
                                    for all entities on the set who
                                    cannot be spoken with. They are
                                    responsible for the care and control
                                    of items and animals, and must
                                    have an expertise in dealing with
                                    these particular items or animals.

About the Author

Bob Moss is a graduate of Northwestern University (Ph.B., 1966) and I.I.T. Chicago Kent College of Law (J.D., 1973). Following a career as a social worker, lawyer, and state district judge, Bob retired and began studying about film—his passion. Bob is a member of the Osher Lifelong Learning Institute (OLLI) at Northwestern University in Chicago. Over the past several years, he has coordinated several film-study groups at OLLI on topics such as *The Art of Watching Films*, *Scene by Scene*, which features directors and actors discussing their famous scenes, and *The Story of Film*. In addition, Bob leads a number of biweekly movie-discussion groups in which the members analyze current feature films and conducts monthly post-screening discussions at his favorite "art" movie theatre in Chicago. This book came about due to the positive response Bob received from the discussion group members who learned how to use the film-analysis technique to which he had guided them.

Reach Bob Moss at:
bob.moss@vibesfromthescreen.com

Follow Bob's blog at:
www.vibesfromthescreen.com